THE STORY OF MEXICO

The
Mexican-American
War

THE STORY OF MEXICO

The
Mexican-American
War

R. CONRAD STEIN

MORGAN
REYNOLDS
PUBLISHING

Greensboro, North Carolina

The Story of Mexico: Mexican-American War

Copyright © 2012 by R. Conrad Stein

Morgan Reynolds Publishing, Inc.
620 South Elm Street, Suite 387
Greensboro, NC 27406 USA

Library of Congress Cataloging-in-Publication Data

Stein, R. Conrad.
 The story of Mexico : Mexican-American War / by R. Conrad Stein.
   p. cm.
 Includes bibliographical references.
 ISBN 978-1-59935-160-5
 1. Mexican War, 1846-1848--Juvenile literature. I. Title.
 E404.S74 2012
 973.6'2--dc22

                               2010041378

Printed in the United States of America
First Edition

Book Cover and interior designed by:
Ed Morgan, navyblue design studio
Greensboro, N.C.

For my wife, Deborah, and daughter, Janna

THE STORY OF MEXICO

TABLE OF CONTENTS

General Augustín de Iturbide

CHAPTER 1

Independence: Triumph and Tragedy

On September 27, 1821, a military band played martial music as a revolutionary army marched into Mexico City. Leading the parade was General Augustín de Iturbide, the country's new chief. The general rode a tall, black horse and sat on a saddle bedecked with silver carvings and sparkling diamonds. Cheering crowds lined the sidewalks, children spread flowers on the street, and elegantly dressed women stood on their balconies waving handkerchiefs at the marchers.

The great parade marked the end of more than ten years of bitter warfare, and it hailed the beginning of the independent state of Mexico. Three centuries of Spanish rule were over; a new nation was born. But despite the music and the waving flags, the scars of war remained in the hearts of the people. As many as 500,000 men and women—almost one-tenth of the nation's total population—had been killed during the war with Spain. Mexican historian Justo Sierra called the conflict "a war without mercy . . . suffocated in blood."

Moreover, independence did not make Mexico a unified nation, as its leaders had once hoped. Instead, the Mexicans were deeply divided along racial and class lines. Indians and mixed-race people mistrusted each other, and both groups mistrusted the whites. The few rich Mexicans lived in fear of an uprising by the legions of poor. These problems—racial hatred and widespread poverty—had existed for centuries under Spanish rule. Independence brought no remedies to the nation's major ills.

The revolutionary war began in 1810 with the high-minded ideals of Catholic priest Miguel Hidalgo. The cause of independence was later taken up by another priest, José María Morelos. Both men had hoped to establish a new society based on democracy, equality of the races, and economic opportunities for all. During the fighting, the two priests were captured and executed by Spanish authorities. Their dreams of a greater Mexico died with them.

By 1821, the old Mexican ruling class, which had been aligned with Spain, controlled the government. Even General Iturbide, who now celebrated independence and freedom from foreign rule, had fought for Spain at the start of the war. After he gained the highest office in the land, Iturbide instructed his followers to call him "Emperor," and he demanded to be treated with the respect and adoration of an Old World king.

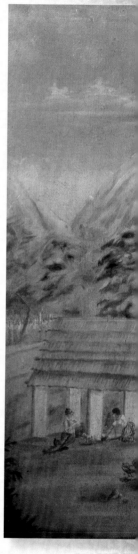

An artist's impression of General O'Donoju Novella and
D'Augustin de Iturbide in 1821 on the Day of the Three Guarantees

Mexican Independence Day

Modern Independence Day celebrations in Mexico focus on the heroic beginning of the revolution against Spain rather than its disappointing end. Independence Day is held every September 16. On that day in 1810, Father Miguel Hidalgo gathered his parishioners in front of his church in the town of Dolores and made an impassioned speech. That speech, now called the *Grito de Hidalgo* (Cry of Hidalgo), filled the people with spirit and sent them marching off to war. Today, in cities and towns all over the country, Mexicans gather at their central plaza on the night of September 15. There the mayor or some other spokesperson attempts to recreate the Cry of Hidalgo. At the end of the speech, fireworks burst in the sky, people shout "Viva Mexico," a band plays, and all sing the National Anthem. The next day, Independence Day, is devoted to parades and demonstrations of patriotism. Independence Day is a spirited time, and its celebration always inspires Mexicans and visitors to the country.

A municipal president giving the *Grito de Hidalgo* at Independence Day festivities

Independent Mexico faced a host of problems, but in 1821 few leaders believed its most immediate threat would be war with the United States. In fact, many Mexican intellectuals at the time saw a bright future for the two countries. Some forty years earlier, the United States had achieved its independence from Great Britain. Enlightened Mexicans hoped that the neighboring nations, both of them republics that had cast off the yoke of colonial rule by a European power, would forge a harmonious partnership in the Americas. Instead, Mexico and the United States were on a collision course. Land, race, and religion were prime causes for the future conflict. And of these, land was the most immediate triggering point.

A vintage map of Mexico dated 1821

CHAPTER 2

The Northern Frontier and an Aggressive Neighbor

When Mexico achieved its independence, it was a land giant, comparable to today's Brazil or Canada. Its territory extended from present-day Guatemala in the south to what is now the southwestern portion of the United States—including Texas and California. Much of this vast area had few Mexican settlements. The population was concentrated in the middle of the country in what was generally called the heartland—a band about two hundred miles wide, centered around Mexico City, and stretching from the Atlantic to the Pacific. Jagged mountain ranges, sprawling deserts, and a lack of navigatable rivers discouraged people from spreading out and building communities beyond this Mexican heartland.

Of all the sparsely populated areas of Mexico, none was more lonely than the huge tract of land called the Northern Frontier. This frontier territory lay above the *Rio Grande* (Big River), which the Spaniards called the *Rio Bravo* (Angry River).

Mexico's Northern Frontier

In all, Mexico's Northern Frontier covered more than 500,000 square miles. The Northern Frontier's borders were ill defined, but they included the present-day American states of Texas, New Mexico, Arizona, and California and parts of what are now Oklahoma, Colorado, Utah, and Nevada.

Mexican claims on this northern land were centuries old. In 1521, Spanish armies commanded by Hernán Cortés defeated the mighty Aztec nation, which was headquartered in present-day Mexico City. After the conquest, Mexico City served as the capital for a colony that the Europeans called New Spain.

In 1540, New Spain sent Francisco Vásques de Coronado and a large party north on an exploration mission. It was the first Spanish venture north of the Rio Grande, which today marks the boundary between Mexico and the United States. So little was known about the north that Coronado chased a legend. According to lore, the northern lands held seven cities of gold, which were so rich that even their poorest inhabitants ate from solid gold dinner plates. Because Coronado hoped to discover the treasures Cortés had encountered years earlier in Mexico, he called the northern region Nueva Mexico, or New Mexico. Coronado never found the fabulous golden cities, but he and his soldiers stood in awe at one of the world's greatest natural treasures: they were the first Europeans to see the Grand Canyon of Arizona.

Settlement of the Northern Frontier began in 1598 when a high-ranking Spaniard named Juan de Oñate took a group of colonists to New Mexico. New Spain was a multiracial society, and the colonists included white Spaniards, Native Americans, and the new race—the mestizos—which was born in New Spain through the union between Native Americans and Europeans. Always, a white Spaniard was in charge of large-scale projects, such as founding colonies on new land. Eventually, the colonists from New Spain built several permanent villages in the New Mexico region of the Northern Frontier.

Before the Pilgrims

Years ago, generations of American schoolchildren were taught that their country began in 1620 when the Pilgrims established Plymouth Rock as the first permanent European settlement in what would become the United States. Those teachings were wrong. They were based on the fact that English-speaking people usually wrote American history books and showed a bias for the English colonists who came over on the *Mayflower*. In truth, Spanish-speaking people from New Spain built towns in what is now the state of New Mexico before the Pilgrims arrived. Santa Fe, New Mexico, was founded in 1608, twelve years prior to the *Mayflower* voyage. In 1610, the Spaniards named Santa Fe the capital of New Mexico.

New Mexico was the first region in the Northern Frontier settled by people from New Spain. In their new lands, the colonists encountered Native American groups, some of which lived in permanent villages while others were nomadic. The Spaniards called the village-dwellers Pueblos after the Spanish word for *towns*. To this day, descendants of the settled tribes in the American Southwest are known as the Pueblo Indians. Spaniards befriended the various Pueblo tribes, but they lived in conflict with the nomads. Eventually, the Pueblos and Spaniards became military allies and fought side by side against nomadic raiding parties.

Although the Pueblos of New Mexico were thought of as friends, authorities from New Spain still imposed harsh rules on them. The Native Americans were told that they were now citizens of New Spain and therefore must abide by laws issued by the Spanish king. Foremost of those laws required them to convert to the Catholic religion and cease worshiping their old gods. In 1680, a dynamic Pueblo chief named Popé, believing he was inspired by the ancient gods, led his people in rebellion against Spanish rule. In a terrible battle, some four hundred New Spain colonists were killed. Popé and his band captured Santa Fe and held the capital for a dozen years. Finally, the rebel Pueblos surrendered and allowed the colonists to reenter their city.

Our Lady of the Rosary, The Unifier

While in exile, the Spanish colonists prayed to a three-foot-tall wooden statue of the Virgin Mary. Upon reentering Santa Fe, the Spaniards gave thanks to the statue for the miracle of victory, and they called it Our Lady of the Rosary, The Conqueror. To this day, the statue is preserved and displayed in the chapel of Santa Fe's Cathedral of Saint Francis. During Corpus Christi Day celebrations, it is paraded through the streets on a special float. The statue is now called Our Lady of the Rosary, The Unifier.

The Cathedral of St. Francis
in Santa Fe, New Mexico

From New Mexico, the colonists spread out east and west. To the east they met a Native American group whose word for friends was *tejas*. In the Spanish language, the word and later the region became Texas. California was so distant from the New Spain heartland that people thought of it as an overseas province since it could be reached far easier by sea rather than through an overland trek. Early Spanish sailors thought California was an island and named it after a mythical treasure island that was mentioned in a novel popular in the 1500s.

Colonists in the Northern Frontier lived in isolation from the rest of New Spain. A journey from Mexico City to Santa Fe, New Mexico, took more than six months. Travelers to all regions of the Northern Frontier had to cross deserts, climb jagged mountains, and always be wary of potentially hostile Indians. Because of these difficulties, few people from New Spain ventured north. As late as 1800, only about 40,000 New Spain citizens lived in the entire Northern Frontier. Even government leaders called the Northern Frontier *tierra despoblado*, or unpopulated lands. Remote California was so underpopulated that judges in New Spain, hoping to settle the region, sent prisoners to work there as part of their punishment.

While the Northern Frontier was isolated from the rest of New Spain, this situation often broadened into splendid isolation. People in the north developed their own culture, their own ways of life, and their own methods of having fun.

In New Mexico, the most populated of the Northern Frontier regions, the settlers lived with a foot in two worlds: Indian and Spanish. New Mexicans discarded the European preference for bread and instead ate corn, the staple of the Indian diet. Corn was consumed in pancake-size servings that the Spaniards called tortillas, or it was mixed with meat to form small cakes called tamales.

When sick, the Spaniards of New Mexico visited Indian doctors, who prescribed herbal teas designed to cure upset stomachs, chronic headaches, and other illnesses. The Indian doctors also chanted over their sick patients in order to chase away the demons of illness.

The Catholic Spaniards accepted these incantations. Young Pueblos and Spaniards freely intermarried. Class rather than race held sway in such unions. A rich Spaniard had no objections to his son marrying an Indian girl, but he hoped the bride-to-be would be a Pueblo princess rather than a commoner.

All New Mexicans tried to attend the annual trade fair held in the northern Mexican city of Chihuahua. For Santa Fe residents, going to the fair meant a six- to eight-week journey over forbidding territory, but families made the trek despite its hardships. At the fair, they looked over luxury goods rarely seen in remote New Mexico—perfumes, fancy handkerchiefs, dresses, and stockings. Even the settlers' enemies, the Navajo Indians, were invited to the trade show. Navajos made superbly woven woolen blankets, which were a coveted trade item.

A Navajo woman weaves a blanket on a vertical loom in this photograph from the early twentieth century.

Music was a passion in the Northern Frontier. Lively Spanish dances, called fandangos, were held regularly in every village. Jail inmates were released during fandango time so that they too could attend the dances. Compassion did not rule the decision to release the prisoners; instead, the jail guards refused to stay on duty and miss the fun of the fandango. In the sleepy town of Los Angeles, California, it was custom for the first person out of his or her house in the morning to sing a well-known song. The next person up and about joined the song in progress, followed by the next and the next. Soon the whole village was locked in a marvelous chorus.

In Texas, which was from the beginning cattle country, the cowboys developed a game similar to football. Played on horseback, the game required a team to advance a watermelon, which served as a ball, by handing it from one rider to another. This watermelon game was a favorite among Texas cowboys, vaqueros, who worked on cattle ranches. Many of the vaqueros were American Indians who had been taught horse riding by settlers. Once in the saddle, the Indian cowboys astonished their instructors by becoming expert riders.

California was a prosperous though sparsely populated region under New Spain. Crops grew well in the pleasant climate, and cattle ranches thrived. Spanish settlers in California, called *Californios*, were famous for their marvelous skills as horse riders. The *Californios* of old loved their horses as much as residents of today's American states are attached to their automobiles. A historian once said of the people, "the saddle was [their] home, the horse a second self."

The most enduring monuments put up by people of the Northern Frontier were the California mission churches. Starting in 1769, Catholic priests built twenty-one such missions along a coastal road, called the *Camino Real* (Royal Road), which stretched the length of California. Each mission was roughly one day's walk to the next. In the mission churches, Indian people heard sermons about Christianity delivered by priests. Missions were also trade schools where Native Americans learned farming techniques that were practiced in Europe.

The twenty-one mission churches have been preserved, and they are the pride of California history enthusiasts today.

Because of its remoteness, colonists in the Northern Frontier had little contact with the heartland of New Spain. When New Spain became Mexico as the result of the War of Independence, the change hardly altered the way of life for people in Texas, New Mexico, and California. However, the old ways would soon die because of a land-hungry neighbor: the United States.

The United States had achieved its independence from England in 1783 with the Treaty of Paris, which ended the Revolutionary War and established a new nation. Even at that early date, the country had started its western expansion. The original thirteen English colonies lay between the Atlantic Ocean to the east and the Appalachian Mountains to the west. The Appalachians were the country's first barrier to cross, although the mountain range proved no great hurdle for hardy American pioneers.

Next came the lands along the Mississippi River, which were collectively called the Louisiana Territory and were claimed by France. President Thomas Jefferson bought this land from the French in 1803 in a gigantic land sale known as the Louisiana Purchase. The Louisiana Purchase almost doubled the size of the United States. Still, the Americans looked farther west, beyond the plains and the mountains to the Pacific Ocean. They dreamed of forging a nation that spread from sea to shining sea.

The spirit behind this westward expansion was called manifest destiny. The word *manifest* in this case should be read as *obvious*. From the American point of view, it was obvious that the U.S. would eventually reach the Pacific. Americans felt that other nations should simply accept this as an established fact. National security, the aggressive American personality, and even divine will were cited as reasons justifying the march westward.

Security demanded expansion because European powers, such as Russia and Great Britain, already eyed the lonely coasts of California and had designs of building colonies there. American restlessness and

This 1872 painting by artist John Gast depicts a woman named Columbia. Columbia holds a school book in her right hand, while using her left to string telegraph wire that will bind the nation's east and west coasts. Titled *American Progress*, the painting also shows Indians, buffalo, and bears fleeing as Columbia leads American settlers westward.

the unstoppable pioneer spirit also meant that the nation's people would move westward regardless of consequences. Only the sea could stop the American pioneers. Finally, many Americans concluded it was God's will that the United States spread across the continent. God blessed the young nation, and God would certainly lead the pioneers to westward conquest. It was as if a Western Star hung in the sky, luring Americans toward its divine light and promising them heaven when they arrived.

Manifest Destiny

Manifest destiny, meaning America's relentless drive to the western lands, was a force from the beginnings of the nation. However, the term did not come into general use until 1845, when magazine editor John L. O'Sullivan said it was "our *manifest destiny* to overspread the continent. . . ." At the time, O'Sullivan was writing an article urging Congress to annex Texas.

The fact that the lands in the West legally belonged to Mexico and made up that country's Northern Frontier meant little to Americans possessed by the spirit of manifest destiny. Americans thought of the West as "empty" land, where only dark-skinned American Indians and a few Mexican settlers lived. Therefore, the West was open and free for white Americans coming from the East. This was true because God commanded it to be true.

For many, the American effort to settle the West—God's work—should start with Texas.

CHAPTER 3

Troubled Texas

In 1820, Moses Austin made the long and difficult journey from Missouri to Texas. Though an American, he was not an enthusiastic proponent of manifest destiny. Austin was instead a fifty-nine-year-old businessman who had recently gone bankrupt because of an investment in a failed lead mine. Now Austin looked for new opportunities and financial rebirth in the little-known land called Texas.

As he entered Texas from the north, Austin noted the wild grasses that towered higher than his horse's head. He passed over clear running rivers and gazed upward at giant pecan trees, rich with nuts, growing on their banks. Deer grazed everywhere. Great herds of buffalo darkened the plains. Austin was not a farmer, but the rich soil of Texas excited him with the possibilities that someday farms and cattle ranches would thrive there.

Of course, Austin knew this land belonged to the king of Spain. He had no intention of settling illegally on the king's property, as had dozens of other Americans in the previous few years. Instead, he planned to ask the authorities of New Spain for a land grant in a perfectly proper manner. He wished to become a citizen of New Spain, sell land to immigrants from the United States, and develop a farming society in Texas. This plan, he reasoned, would benefit New Spain as well as it would benefit Moses Austin. Leaders in New Spain were painfully aware that Texas stood as the next step in the American march westward. A large group of American farmers, who swore loyalty to the king of Spain, would perhaps stand as a wall and thwart expansion by their countrymen.

Two developments foiled the planned farming community. First, Mexico won its war with Spain and became an independent nation in 1821. Second, Moses Austin died after contracting pneumonia that same year. The dream of establishing a Texas colony now fell to his son, Stephen.

Stephen Austin, a bachelor in his mid-twenties, did not share his father's passion for the future of Texas. He was a bookish young man and a music lover who enjoyed playing his flute as a member of a symphony orchestra. He preferred city life to country living, and the prospect of building a frontier community in the wilds of Texas had little appeal to him. Stephen was by training a banker. He too had suffered business reversals and was in debt. Despite his misgivings, Stephen decided to journey to Texas and see for himself the land that had so captured his father's imagination. Upon arriving in Texas he was, like his father, impressed. In a letter, he claimed the land was "as good in every respect as a man could wish for, land first rate, plenty of timber, fine water—beautiful rolling."

In the late summer of 1821, Stephen Austin entered the village of San Antonio, the capital of the province of Texas. Undoubtedly, he saw a prominent church with thick walls enclosing a courtyard. That church was popularly called the Alamo after the cottonwood trees (*alamo* trees in Spanish) that surrounded its grounds. In the capital city, he pursued his father's goals, signing papers and meeting with Mexican government heads. To his delight, he was given a large grant of well-watered land along the Brazos River in southeastern Texas. This was some of the finest farmland in the whole region.

The Father of Texas

Stephen Austin is today hailed as "The Father of Texas." Austin, the capital city of modern Texas, is named in his honor.

As his father had planned, Stephen divided his land into parcels and distributed them to responsible citizens of the United States. The first families to whom Stephen granted land titles are today called the Old 300, although in actual fact there were 297 such families. From the beginning, the Old 300 were deemed by Stephen to be sensible and responsible people. Austin was familiar with American frontier settlements in his native Missouri, and he did not want to duplicate them in Texas. He considered American frontier communities to be dirty, rowdy, and boisterous. Austin interviewed those applying for land, and he wrote a set of rules: "no frontiersman who has no other occupation than that of hunter will be received—no drunkard, no gambler, no profane swearer, no idler." The normally mild-mannered Austin enforced these rules. On more than one occasion, he ordered drunken men who acted wildly to be tied to a post and whipped.

All of Austin's Old 300 colonists agreed to comply with Mexican law, which required them to learn the Spanish language and to convert to the Catholic religion. However, there was no police force or courts in Texas to ensure that these laws were carried out. Few of the settlers made a serious attempt to learn Spanish, and fewer still became Catholics.

Of all the Mexican laws applicable to the Texas settlers, none were more daunting than those dealing with slavery. Most of the early settlers from the United States were Southerners, and many brought slaves with them to Texas. The Mexican government disapproved of slavery, but the American settlers in Texas resisted any restrictions on their slave-owning practices. Their attitude was similar to that which prevailed in the Southern states: slaves were "property," and no government should deny a citizen of his or her "goods." By 1825, a census of Austin's colony in Texas counted 443 slaves and 1,347 free whites.

Slaves toiling in Texas were aware that their owners lived in conflict with their new government. The enslaved men and women learned that if they escaped and trekked south of the Rio Grande, the government of Mexico would do nothing to apprehend them and return them to their owners. According to one Mexican official, this knowledge made the slaves eager "to throw off their yokes, while their masters believe they can keep them by making [the yoke] heavier. They commit the barbarities on their slaves . . . they pull their teeth, they set dogs upon them to tear them apart and the mildest of them will whip the slaves until they are flayed."

While the American settlers carved out their own colony in Texas, chaos reigned in Mexico City. The Mexican people had little experience with self-rule because for three hundred years Spain had controlled their government with a heavy hand. All decisions had been made by the faraway king. To disobey the king had meant swift punishment, perhaps the death penalty. Now the suddenly independent people were forced to make their own decisions and form a government without the benefit of building from a foundation. The process seemed to baffle them. Even under Spain, the Mexicans had been a deeply divided people, and now a weak central government brought those divisions roaring to the surface.

Division between the races remained. Whites held the money and the political power, mixed-race people (mestizos) were given minor privileges, and Indians were treated almost as a foreign race within their own country. Politically, the Mexicans were split into two broad categories: the liberals who hoped to change the system and the conservatives who longed for the "orderliness" of Spanish rule. Moreover, two classes of men, the military and the church, demanded and usually received special privileges from the government.

Augustín de Iturbide, the first head of independent Mexico and the self-proclaimed "emperor" of the country, lasted in office only about ten months before he was overthrown by rivals and forced to flee to Europe. Later, Iturbide made the mistake of returning to Mexico. He was promptly arrested, lined up against a wall, and executed by a firing squad. His fate mirrored that of many Mexican chiefs. In the first three decades of independence, Mexico had fifty different governments. Presidents came and went not through orderly elections, but due to coups, counter-coups, and army rebellions. Not even scholars in Mexican history can list the names of all the government heads who served during that bewildering initial stage of the republic.

Yet one name—Antonio López de Santa Anna—stands out. Santa Anna was a white man of European heritage who had been born into a wealthy family. When only a teenager, he became an army officer. Early in the War of Independence, he fought for the side that favored the continuation of Spanish rule. When it seemed clear that the independents would win the war, he joined them and became a nationalist. He would repeat this pattern throughout his life—testing political winds, switching loyalties at will, and never missing an opportunity to advance. He was a liberal when it suited him. He was a conservative when it suited him.

Santa Anna was never trusted by honest Mexicans, but given the turmoil of post-independence, he represented the only figure people could turn to. He always survived and often thrived during times of upheaval. From 1833 to 1855, Santa Anna was Mexico's president eleven different times. When he was not in political office, he was leading armies in the field as Mexico's top general. Driving ambition ruled his personality. He was once heard to say, "Were I made God, I should wish to be something more."

As a commander, Santa Anna was gifted with military talent. In 1825, naval forces from Spain seized the port city of Tampico in an attempt to reimpose colonial rule over Mexico. The Spanish troops were immediately weakened by an outbreak of yellow fever, a dreaded disease called the *vomito negro* (black vomit). Santa Anna led an army to Tampico. Before the mission, he carefully screened his men, choosing only those who were native to the Tampico region and therefore had some immunities to yellow fever. At the port city, Santa Anna had little trouble defeating the sickened Spanish soldiers. Because of his victory, the general was hailed as the "Hero of Tampico."

In sharp contrast to the confusion in Mexico, the United States had a stable government and no crises in leadership. One issue, the divisive problem of slavery, lay in the background burning like a smoldering fire. But early in the 1800s, the slavery question had yet

Antonio López de Santa Anna

The beauty and fertility of Texas land was intoxicating to settlers.

to tear the nation apart. Instead, a feeling of excitement charged the air. New inventions such as railroads and the telegraph promised to revolutionize American life. Citizens marched steadily westward as if answering God's calling.

All eyes focused on Texas, the free land, the empty land to the west. Intoxicated by the promise of their future, Americans refused to recognize that Texas legally belonged to Mexico and instead thought the region was theirs for the taking. Manifest destiny ruled American thinking and overwhelmed any notions of respect for the rights of its southern neighbor.

By the late 1820s, Americans migrated to Texas at the rate of 10,000 a year. Many came from the log cabin communities in Kentucky and Tennessee. They boarded up their cabins, painted the letters G.T.T. (which stood for "Gone to Texas") on the door, and headed west. These were not the kind of dignified and refined people Stephen

Austin had once sought for his colony. In fact, most of the newcomers had no intention of joining Austin's group. Some of the migrants were fugitives from justice and went to Texas to escape jail terms. Legally or illegally, they established farms in Texas where they saw fit and defended their holdings with guns if necessary.

While American pioneers grabbed land that belonged to Mexico, leaders in the United States government stood silent. Many congressmen believed Mexico's Northern Frontier would fall to the Americans some day, but in the 1820s few voiced that belief for fear of provoking war. This situation changed when Washington authorities appointed Joel R. Poinsett as the first American minister to independent Mexico. Poinsett had lived in Latin America and spoke Spanish well—perhaps too well. He was outspoken about American demands on Mexico's Northern Frontier. He was also a meddler who dabbled in Mexican politics and worked to enhance the power of the liberal factions.

In Mexico City, Poinsett had an audience with General Santa Anna. The conversation took place in the early 1820s, years before Santa Anna's rise to prominence. The exchange illustrated the general's ambitions as well as his contempt for his countrymen. According to Poinsett, Santa Anna told him, "A hundred years to come, my people will [still] not be fit for liberty. They do not know what it is, unenlightened as they are, and under the influence of a Catholic clergy; a despotism is the proper government for them, but there is no reason why it should not be a wise and virtuous one." The general made it clear that he—Antonio López de Santa Anna—would be the ideal "wise and virtuous" despot to run the nation.

In a speech to Mexican congressmen, Poinsett shocked his audience by suggesting the country ought to sell Texas to the United States. After all, he explained, there were few Mexican settlers in Texas and the land there was going to waste. Poinsett clearly did not understand Mexican sensitivities concerning the country's sovereignty. Mexican territory was sacred to the people. Despite Mexico's deep divisions, all parties agreed that the nation should never surrender, sell, or transfer a mile of land to the United States. Poinsett's speech put Mexicans on the alert. Now they believed that the leaders in Washington, not just the land-hungry pioneers, coveted Mexican territory.

The Diplomat and the Flower

Joel Roberts Poinsett was a tactless diplomat, but he possessed skills as a botanist. While in Mexico, he discovered an attractive flower that he named after himself, the poinsettia. He brought the flower home with him, and the pretty poinsettia became one of the most popular house and garden plants in the United States.

By the end of the 1820s, Americans in Texas outnumbered Mexicans more than ten to one. They gathered in English-speaking communities where they called themselves not Americans, not Mexicans, but Texans—sometimes pronounced and spelled Texians. The Texans established their own schools, while the Mexicans in the territory had none. They kept slaves and worshiped in non-Catholic churches—both violations of Mexican law.

In order to regain control of Texas, the Mexican government passed a series of laws designed to curtail American influence. Further immigration to Texas was outlawed. Anti-slavery measures were enforced. Settlers in Texas were forbidden to trade goods with any nation other than Mexico. All these laws infuriated the Texans. To give the laws teeth, the government sent a large army unit to Texas. The presence of the army made a tense situation explosive. Mexican soldiers, as had long been their custom in Mexico proper, bullied citizens, arrested them without cause, and levied excessive fines.

Hoping to bring a measure of calm to the situation, Stephen Austin traveled to Mexico City. He could not speak for all the settlers, but he was a well-respected man among the Americans in Texas. At this point, Austin was still determined to be a proper citizen of Mexico and work within the country's laws. He conferred with several leaders, including General Santa Anna. Austin left Mexico City believing he had made accords with Mexican authorities, and he hoped peace would prevail in Texas.

In Northern Mexico, Stephen Austin was suddenly arrested. He was taken back to Mexico City, where he was jailed. He was never formally accused of a crime and he never saw a judge. The Texans, hearing of their leader's plight, protested but to no avail. Austin was held in prison for eighteen months, all the time growing bitter against his captors. When he was finally released, Austin returned to Texas and spoke before a local militia group made up of angry Texans. "War is our only resource," he said. "There is no other remedy. We must defend our rights, ourselves, and our country by force of arms."

In 1832, an American rode into Texas. Unlike the most recent migrants, this man was wealthy and well educated. In fact, just a few years earlier he had been considered a candidate to run for president of the United States. He was Sam Houston, a war hero, a one-time congressman, and a former governor of Tennessee.

Houston was despondent because his wife and he had quarreled and split up. He spent several years with the Cherokee Indians, his favorite people, while trying to recover his spirits. Finally, Houston decided to move to Texas. While riding into the territory, he was overwhelmed by what he interpreted to be a spiritual event. "An eagle swooped down near my head, and then, soaring aloft with wildest screams, was lost in the rays of the setting sun," he recalled. "I knew that a great destiny waited for me in the West."

Samuel Houston

Along with Stephen Austin, Sam Houston is a famous Texas pioneer. The city of Houston is named for him. After Texas achieved statehood, Houston served as its governor and its senator. He resigned as governor in 1861 because his state was drifting toward the South in the Civil War, and he disagreed with Confederate policies.

Houston entered Texas as the region teetered on the brink of war. Many American settlers still spoke of seeking reform within the government of Mexico. However, a growing and vocal faction advocated separating Texas from Mexico and seeking an alliance with the United States even if such a move meant war with Mexico. Also, some of the colonists who were ethnic Mexicans opposed their unstable government and sided with the Texans. Sam Houston took charge of the settlers who aimed toward independence.

The first military confrontation between Texans and the Mexican army occurred on October 2, 1835, in the town of Gonzales. A militia group in the town had been given a small cannon to help in the defense of Indian raids. Now the Mexican army, fearing a rebellion in Texas, wanted the cannon back. The Texans refused. About 160 settlers, armed with hunting guns, stood in front of the cannon and dared a Mexican army unit to try to haul it away. Over the cannon, someone raised a banner that boldly declared "COME AND TAKE IT." A brief gunfight broke out and the Mexican army unit, consisting of about one hundred soldiers, retreated. The Texans celebrated their victory. It marked the first battle in the Texas Revolution, and—history would prove—the first skirmish of the Mexican-American War.

As war brewed in Texas, both sides had grave issues against each other. Mexicans looked upon the Texans as an ungrateful, slave-owning people who accepted Mexico's gift of land and then turned against a generous government. Texans saw the Mexican government as a dictatorship that would force them to change their religion and would deny them their freedom—even though one of the "freedoms" they jealously guarded was their "freedom" to own slaves.

Stephen Austin journeyed to Washington to try to enlist the support of President Andrew Jackson. Meanwhile, several famous Americans came to Texas to join what they believed was a patriotic cause. One was Jim Bowie, a rugged frontiersman famous for developing the Bowie knife, which had a cutting edge on both the bottom and the top of its blade. Bowie's wife and two children had recently died in

A Union soldier with a large Bowie knife
on his belt during the Civil War

a cholera epidemic and now, despondent, he was drowning himself in whiskey. Another was Davy Crockett, a pioneer and a congressman from Tennessee who had become an American folk hero. Friends said Davy Crockett could aim his rifle at a lighted candlewick and shoot it out at a distance of three hundred feet. Also arriving in Texas was William Travis, an idealistic lawyer and army officer who hailed from South Carolina. Travis was wanted by the law because he had killed an Alabama man before escaping to Texas.

Travis took command of about 150 Texans, including Crocket and Bowie. This small band determined that they would defend the city of San Antonio from the Mexican army. In marched General Antonio López de Santa Anna, leading a force of about 5,000 men. Santa Anna longed for a complete victory in San Antonio because he once again had his eyes on the presidency and wanted to return to Mexico City bragging of his triumph over the Americans. Before leaving Mexico, the general declared, "I personally will march forth to subdue the rebels, and, once this is done, my cannon will establish the boundary between Mexico and the United States."

In the town of San Antonio, William Travis led his followers to the walled courtyard of the church called the Alamo. A storied chapter of American history was about to be written. Outside the walls, Santa Anna ordered his buglers to play a grim song with a wild rhythm—the "*Deguello*," also known as "The Fire and Death Song." His soldiers flew a blood red flag. The flag and the song were ancient symbols that indicated to the Alamo defenders that he intended to take no prisoners.

Line in the Sand

A legend says that William Travis, knowing his force was hopelessly outnumbered at the Alamo, gathered the defenders in front of him and drew a line in the sand with his sword. He announced that anyone who wished to escape and try to find safety beyond the Mexican ranks should cross the line immediately. If they did, they would be free to go. According to the story, only one man chose to escape. This "Line in the Sand" tale has been told and retold over the generations. There is no way to confirm if it is fact or fiction.

After a long artillery barrage, Santa Anna ordered his men to charge. Shouts rang out from the ranks: *"Viva, Mexico! Viva, Santa Anna!"* Travis and the defenders stayed behind the Alamo's thick walls, which stood twelve feet high. The Texans, most of whom were superb shots, cut down the Mexicans as they advanced. "I can tell you the whole scene was one of extreme terror," a Mexican soldier wrote later.

The battle, which took place on March 6, 1836, lasted ninety hellish minutes. Mexican soldiers, braving death, pressed forward to the Alamo's walls. Those in the front ranks slammed ladders against the walls, and soldiers scrambled upward. Said one attacking soldier, "The first to climb were thrown down by bayonets or by pistol fire, but others hurried to occupy their places, climbing over their bleeding bodies." Inside, using their muskets as clubs, the defenders fought back. All the Texans were killed. Some reports say that several Texans surrendered, but Santa Anna order them bayoneted.

The Alamo, in San Antonio, Texas. More than 2.5 million visitors from all over the world visit the site each year, making it Texas's premier tourist attraction.

Weeks after the Alamo battle, Colonel Nicolás de la Portilla, an assistant to Santa Anna, surrounded a force of 330 Texans near the town of Goliad. The Texans surrendered, and at first Portilla decided to treat them honorably as prisoners of war. Then a note arrived from Santa Anna ordering him to execute the captives. Portilla agonized over his decision. Finally, he obeyed his commander, and the Texans were herded together in ranks, forced to kneel, and gunned down. About sixty of the 330 Texans escaped with their lives in the smoke of gunfire.

Word of the massacres at Goliad and the Alamo spread terror throughout the Texas settlements. Farm families stopped their work and fled east toward United States territory. One settler, Noah Smithwick, wrote, "Houses were standing open, the beds unmade, the breakfast things still on the table . . . all abandoned." This sort of panic was the reaction Santa Anna had hoped to provoke. He wanted his brutal battle tactics to trigger a stampede of frightened colonists out of Texas because an empty territory would be easier to conquer.

After the initial shock, however, the mood of the Texans turned from fear to rage. Men swore vengeance against the slaughters at the Alamo and at Goliad. Near the town of Gonzales, Sam Houston commanded a Texan militia unit of about nine hundred volunteers, all of whom sought an immediate fight with Santa Anna. Houston, the only experienced soldier among them, believed his followers were not ready to battle professional Mexican fighting men. He held them back, concentrated on repairing all rifles, and subjected the men to military drills. They objected. All this "playing soldier" made no sense to them while Santa Anna and his army still roamed free in Texas. Some Texans openly called their leader a coward. But Houston was a commanding presence. He stood six feet two inches, a tall man for the times, and he was a brilliant speaker. Gradually, he won the respect and obedience of his militia.

Santa Anna was also eager for a fight. His troops were tired, hungry, and growing fearful in this strange country so far from home. Out of frustration, General Santa Anna defied military common sense and split his force into several commands, ordering his officers to seek out and destroy the Texans.

On April 21, 1836, Santa Anna and about 1,000 troops camped along the banks of the San Jacinto River. Secretly, the Mexican general was being watched by Houston's scouts. Houston waited for the opportune moment to attack. In the afternoon, after their midday meal, the Mexican soldiers rested. They were weary after marching for many days, and the afternoon was the traditional siesta time for Mexicans. Houston, a wily warrior, had studied the habits of his enemy.

In a soft voice, Houston told his men to hold their fire as they approached the Mexican camp. Amazingly, Santa Anna had posted no sentries. The Texans advanced silently to within two hundred yards of the Mexican tents. Then Houston gave the order to charge. With cries of "Remember the Alamo!" and "Remember Goliad!" the Texans rushed forward. What followed was slaughter on a grisly scale. Most Mexicans were asleep with their rifles stacked outside their tents. The Texans killed enemy soldiers with gunfire, bayonets, swords, and even clubs. Many Mexicans tried to surrender but were cut down. An American sergeant wrote, "The most awful slaughter I ever saw was when the Texans pursued the retreating Mexicans, killing on all sides, even the wounded."

When the fighting finally ceased, Sam Houston's forces had killed 630 of the enemy and captured 730 more at the Battle of San Jacinto. His own losses were nine dead and thirty wounded. The Texan victory was complete.

The next day, a group of Texans discovered General Santa Anna hiding in some bushes. Normally, the general was fastidious about his dress. Now he wore a ragged shirt that he apparently had stolen from the clothesline of a settler's cabin. In this rather shameful condition, he was brought before Sam Houston.

Houston was in agony because a bullet had shattered his foot during the previous day's battle. Still, he was aware that thousands of Mexican soldiers commanded by other officers remained in Texas. Houston told Santa Anna to withdraw his troops from Texas immediately.

The Yellow Rose of Texas

Historians have pondered why the Mexicans allowed the Texans to sneak up on their camp undetected at the San Jacinto River. A colorful story holds that General Santa Anna was distracted by an uncommonly beautiful young lady. The lady was Emily West, a mulatto (*yellow* was a slang term for mixed-race people in those days) slave who was mistress to a Texan ranch owner. Santa Anna became enchanted by the slave girl and took her for his mistress. Emily West resented being carried off, and before going with the general she sent a fellow slave to tell Sam Houston where the Mexicans were camped. She then entertained Santa Anna in his tent while Houston and his men silently approached. This tale served as the source for a famous song, "The Yellow Rose of Texas," which was written in the 1830s and taken to the American Civil War by Confederate soldiers. The Civil War version of the song opened with the lines:

There's a yellow rose of Texas
That I am going to see,
No other fellow knows her,
No soldier, only me.
She cried so when I left her,
It like to broke my heart,
And if I ever find her
We never more will part.

He also informed the Mexican general that Texas was now an independent nation and that his government should recognize independence as a fact. Santa Anna, afraid Houston would order him executed, agreed to all of his demands.

The Texas Declaration of Independence

Acting in great haste, a convention met in the Texas town of Washington On The Bravos on March 2, 1836, to write a formal declaration of independence from Mexico. At the time of the writing, the Alamo was under siege by Santa Anna's forces. The Texas Declaration of Independence is modeled after the American Declaration written sixty years earlier. Its first sentence reads, "When a government has ceased to protect the lives, liberty, and property of the people, from whom its legitimate powers are derived, and for the advancement of whose happiness it was instituted, and so far from being a guarantee for the enjoyment of those inestimable and inalienable rights, becomes an instrument in the hands of evil rulers for their oppression."

After the Battle of San Jacinto, a temporary peace prevailed in Texas and between the United States and Mexico. It was a tense peace. Most Mexican leaders believed the entire Texas Revolution was an American plot designed to wrest the region from them. Americans, for their part, held that God demanded they take over all the land between Texas and California. The Mexican-American War did not start until 1846, but historians contend that the actual fighting between the two nations broke out ten years earlier in troubled Texas.

GENERAL D. ANTONIO LOPEZ DE SANTA-ANNA,
PRESIDENT OF THE REPUBLIC OF MEXICO.
By **A. Hoffy**, from an original likeness taken from life at **Vera-Cruz.**

The above is a correct likeness from our personal observation

E. W. Moore

Com'. late Texas Navy.

Alex'. C. Blount

Published July 1847, by **A. HOFFY**, N:º 20, South Third S.t near Chesnut, Philad.ª

& by **JOHNSON & BROCKETT**, N.º 28, South Seventh S.t bet. Chesnut & Walnut.

Entered according to act of Congress in the year 1847 by A. Hoffy & Johnson & Brockett in the Clerks office of the district Court of the Eastern district of Pennsyl.

CHAPTER 4

Two Nations on the Brink

Sam Houston kept General Santa Anna as a prisoner for the next eight months. At one point, he sent Santa Anna to Washington, D.C., to discuss Mexican relations with his old friend, President Andrew Jackson. The talks proved fruitless. Feelings between the United States and Mexico remained stressful. When General Santa Anna was released, he drifted back to Mexico City only to find his countrymen blaming him for the loss of Texas. In disgrace, Santa Anna retired to his large farm in Veracruz. As always, he looked for a proper opportunity to reemerge.

Texas now organized itself as an independent nation. In the nation's first elections, Sam Houston was voted in as president. In that same election, a majority of Texans put it on record that they wished to become a territory of the United States. This move, however, was viewed as tricky business in Washington. Mexico regarded Texas as a rebellious colony, not an independent country. If the U.S. annexed Texas, the act would likely trigger a war with its southern neighbor. Mexico made this issue clear by saying that a U.S. takeover of Texas would be "sufficient [cause] for the immediate proclamation of war."

The Lone Star Nation

For ten years, from 1836 to 1846, the Republic of Texas acted as an independent country. Most citizens of the republic believed they would eventually join the United States, but several advocated that they remain independent. Early in its history, the Republic of Texas adopted a flag with a single star as its national banner. The single star, or *lone star*, symbolized the courage of the Texan people as they made their way alone in the family of nations. To this day, the American state of Texas is nicknamed the Lone Star State.

Meanwhile, the United States was hesitant to act boldly on the Texas matter because the nation suffered its own internal problems. By the 1840s, the fiery issue of slavery deeply divided the American people. Many Northerners suspected that Southerners wanted Texas so they could make it a slave state and therefore enhance their power. The fight over slavery, which for decades had been a war of words, grew more intense with each passing year.

Mexico too was weak due to political upheaval. Liberals and conservatives continued their battles. Several Mexican states threatened to follow the Texas example and break away from the union. Spaniards left the country because the Mexican people tended to blame current problems on their former masters. The Spaniards were the nation's most experienced merchants, and they were replaced by businessmen from the United States, Great Britain, and France. By driving out the Spaniards, the Mexican people exchanged one form of colonialism with another. The influence of foreign businessmen eventually led to trouble.

In 1838, a French cook who owned a pastry shop in Mexico City claimed that his store had been looted by drunken Mexican army officers. The cook appealed to his government, and France demanded

600,000 pesos as compensation for its citizen. The claim was hopelessly exaggerated as the average Mexican worker at the time earned about one peso a day. Nevertheless, the two countries went to war over the incident. The French navy bombarded the fortress of San Juan de Ultía and seized the port city of Veracruz. Mexican intellectuals, who were famous for their cutting satire, dubbed this conflict the Pastry War.

The Pastry War would have been a comic opera event had it not been used as an avenue for the reemergence of Antonio López de Santa Anna. A foreign navy occupied a Mexican city, and national pride was at stake. Santa Anna, with his heightened sense of drama, chose this situation to capture the spotlight. While he led troops into battle near Veracruz, a French cannonball struck Santa Anna in the leg. Doctors examined the shattered leg and determined they had to amputate. Santa Anna, believing he would die, wrote a long farewell letter to his country. The general claimed he had been victorious on the battlefield and now was prepared for death as a happy man. Meanwhile, diplomats promised French officials they would pay the 600,000 pesos (the sum was never paid), and the French fleet sailed away, thus ending the Pastry War.

From his agonizing wound, a new chapter in Santa Anna's life emerged. The general recovered from his injuries. Because he was so badly wounded while defending Mexico, he again won the hearts of his countrymen. Even his severed leg became a national icon. Santa Anna ordered a state funeral for the amputated limb, and it was buried with honors in a mausoleum on his plantation near Veracruz.

Although his popularity was restored, Santa Anna did not immediately seek the presidency. Mexico's president through most of the 1830s was Anastasio Bustamante, an honest if unimaginative official. Bustamante, a conservative, was unable to provide order in the turmoil of post-independence Mexico. In 1840, a liberal rival, Valentín Gómez Farías, led an army revolt against Bustamante. For twelve days, soldiers loyal to the two politicians battled in the streets of Mexico City. The fighting included cannon exchanges, which did little damage to the troops but killed many civilians.

Mexico City's ancient downtown plaza, the Zocalo

Mexicans demanded an end to this anarchy. Intellectuals believed that the North Americans, the hated *Yanquis*, would use the disorder in their country as an excuse to march south and take over. A frustrated Mexican populace asked Santa Anna to once more be their president. The general from Veracruz was happy to answer the call.

In 1842, Santa Anna became Mexico's president for the fifth time. He was aided by a new constitution, which gave the office of president dictatorial powers. Believing he was the only man who could restore order, Mexicans bowed to Santa Anna as if he were a European king. One of his first acts as president was to retrieve his amputated leg from the mausoleum in Veracruz and have it paraded through the main streets of the capital in a magnificent horse-drawn coach. The limb was then reburied with full military honors at a new resting place in the heart of the city. Next the president ordered a huge statue of himself erected in Mexico City's ancient downtown plaza, the Zocalo. The statue showed him pointing north, in the direction of Texas, a land he vowed to reconquer. Critics noted that the statue also pointed across the plaza to the national mint, an institution he often raided for gold and silver.

Santa Anna appointed hundreds of new officers to the Mexican army and gave them all glittering uniforms. Army expenses more than doubled under his leadership. Meanwhile, Mexico lacked an adequate public school system, and its public roads were in deplorable condition. Instead of making progress to give the people better lives, the government of Mexico seemed to be taking giant steps backward.

Difficulties with Texas, the Lone Star Republic, persisted. In September 1842, a unit of three hundred Texas cavalrymen crossed the Rio Grande in pursuit of Mexican soldiers. At the time, Sam Houston was serving his second term as Texas's president, and he had ordered the militia to stay on their own side of the Texas border. The cavalry commander—foolishly, it turned out—disobeyed the order. The three hundred Texans found themselves surrounded by 2,000 Mexican troops, and they were forced to surrender.

At first, Santa Anna wanted all the captives executed, but he was persuaded to relent. Instead, he ordered the Texans to be *decimated*, an ancient form of unit punishment that dated back to the days of Imperial Rome. Decimation meant that one in ten of the prisoners were condemned to be executed. In a grim lottery, the Texans were forced to reach into a deep jar, so deep they could not see the contents, and pick out one bean. Those who came up with a white bean were spared. The unlucky ones who chose a black bean (one in ten were black) were shot.

This murderous chapter in the relationship between Texas and Mexico was later called the Black Bean Episode. It took place in March 1843 near the town of Mier, Mexico, which is some ninety miles northeast of Monterrey. As news of the Black Bean Episode circulated in Texas, the people's hatred toward Mexico grew to a cold fury. A Texas newspaper urged young men to join the militia and "think of our countrymen martyred at the Alamo, at Goliad, at Mier."

Santa Anna continued his lavish ways in office while the fortunes of Mexico sank. The president was a devotee of cockfighting and other forms of gambling. Night after night, he lost fortunes at gaming tables, and he seemed not to care about the vanished funds. When his wife of nineteen years died of an illness, Santa Anna dipped into the treasury to order a state funeral, which attracted 20,000 mourners. Weeks after the funeral, the president, who was fifty, married a fifteen-year-old girl. While the president wasted funds, Mexican government officials went unpaid, the country's foreign debts mounted, Texas remained a colony in rebellion, and friction with the United States was high.

This time, Mexicans blamed the president for the country's dismal situation. Late in 1844, rival generals revolted against Santa Anna and installed José Joaquín Herrera as president. Mexico City mobs celebrated the overthrow by toppling Santa Anna's statue and breaking into the case that held his leg and dragging it through the streets.

Santa Anna fled to Cuba. The new president, Joaquín Herrera, was a skilled administrator, but the nation by this time was ungovernable.

As Mexican intellectuals feared, anarchy in their country prompted the United States to intensify its pressure on gobbling up Texas and the Northern Frontier. In March 1845, U.S. President John Tyler signed a bill authorizing the annexation of Texas. Mexico was far too weak and disorganized to act boldly against the *Yanquis*. In addition, another revolt broke out and Herrera, who lasted only a year as president, was overthrown. A new president, Mariano Paredes, was left to deal with the Americans and face the grim prospect of waging war.

Also in 1845, James K. Polk was inaugurated as the eleventh president of the United States. He was a humorless man who once had been a small-town lawyer. Polk vowed from the beginning that his presidency would be devoted to specific goals, one of which was his country's territorial expansion. In this task, he succeeded brilliantly. Polk could be called the president of manifest destiny.

President James K. Polk

Polk's first step was to acquire the Oregon Country, the vast territory in the Pacific Northwest that today comprises the states of Washington, Oregon, Idaho, and parts of Montana and Wyoming. Great Britain was also interested in the Oregon region, and the two nations almost went to war over the matter. Polk negotiated a boundary line at the 49th parallel (the present border between the U.S. and Canada), and the dispute was settled peacefully. In the Northwest, the United States now stretched to the Pacific. The dreams of manifest destiny had been partially fulfilled.

Next Polk turned to the South. The American president sent his special agent, John Slidell, to Mexico City on a mission to buy California from the Mexican government. Slidell, a Louisiana congressman, was authorized to offer up to $25 million and the forgiveness of all other debts that Mexico owed to the U.S. in exchange for California and New Mexico. Polk wanted land; he did not necessarily want war. However, it was unthinkable for any Mexican president to even consider selling the country's territory to the *Yanquis*. Such an act would cause the people to rise up and force their president out of office. The Mexican government refused to even speak to Polk's special agent. Slidell interpreted the official silence as a personal insult and urged Polk to seek a declaration of war.

The status of California and New Mexico simmered like a stew left too long on the fire. Certainly the stew pot would soon boil over. Neither side appreciated the other's position, making compromise impossible. Mexicans considered the United States to be a bullying power. They asked the question: Would a northern country, say Canada, demand the state of Maine from the United States? Of course not! An American president who would surrender his country's territory would certainly be thrown out of office. This same situation held true for a Mexican president. California and the Northern Frontier were sacred to the Mexican soul. Those lands were not for sale—not at any price.

As it turned out, it was a dispute over Texas that tipped the scales and finally led to war. President Polk acted as if Texas was American territory because of the annexation of 1845. Mexican leaders claimed that Texas was a colony in rebellion and still belonged to the mother country. Polk ignored the Mexican objections. Many historians conclude that President Polk lacked proper respect for Mexican rights, and still others say he disliked Mexican people.

In 1846, the United States already had soldiers stationed in Texas. Local Mexican people called the troops *Yanquis* (Yankees), no matter if the men were from the northern or the southern states The Yankees were commanded by General Zachary Taylor, a forty-year army veteran who had fought many Indian wars. Taylor and his men erected an earthen and timber stockade on the northern banks of the Rio Grande and called it Fort Texas. Building a military facility in this region of Texas was an aggressive act in itself. Critics would later claim that the construction of Fort Texas on the Rio Grande was a deliberate move on Polk's part, an action designed to provoke war. The Rio Grande was not the traditional borderline between Texas and Mexico proper. Most nations recognized the Nueces River, about 150 miles to the north, to be the proper boundary. In fact, in prior dealings with Spain, the U.S. government had respected the Nueces River borderline.

On April 25, 1846, Mexican and American cavalry units fought a brief battle along the Rio Grande not far from Fort Texas. Both sides suffered light casualties. It was little more than a border incident, but President Polk treated this clash as a "smoking gun"—his dramatic reason for war. Polk had already written a speech asking Congress to issue a declaration of war because Mexico had refused to sell its territory. He knew such a refusal was a weak argument for warfare. Then, the night before he was to deliver his speech, news arrived in Washington of the skirmish on the Rio Grande. Now the president changed the wording of that speech. On May 11, 1846, Polk told Congress, "Mexico has passed the boundary of the United States, has

Zachary Taylor

The Rio Grande forms a natural partial border between Mexico and the United States.

invaded our territory, and shed American blood on the American soil. She has proclaimed that hostilities have commenced, and that the two nations are now at war."

Most historians now believe the speech was a cynical act, one designed to mislead. The Rio Grande where "American blood" was shed "on American soil" was a territory in dispute, and certainly Mexico had as many legitimate claims to that soil as did the United States. At the time, Abraham Lincoln was a lawyer from Illinois and was running for a seat in Congress. The future president stated, "It is a fact, that the United States Army, in marching to the Rio Grande, marched into a peaceful Mexican settlement, and frightened the inhabitants away from their homes and growing crops. . . . That soil was not ours; and Congress did not annex it or attempt to annex it."

Despite the misgivings of Lincoln and other Americans, a majority of congressmen agreed with President Polk. Manifest destiny was a passion sweeping the country. Congressmen feared their patriotism, and indeed their manhood, would be called into question if they failed to deliver a declaration. Congress declared war on Mexico on May 13, 1846.

From the beginning, the war was controversial and divisive in the United States. Northerners continued to fear that the South secretly wished to occupy all of Mexico and set up a vast slave society there. Polk was a Southerner and a slaveholder all his life, but he had no grandiose schemes to take over Mexico and bring the practice of slavery to that land. Manifest destiny, his country's expansion to the Pacific, was always his foremost goal. Now that war was upon him, Polk believed the clash with Mexico would be short and not terribly costly in blood. He thought—and perhaps prayed—that after a few U.S. battle victories, the Mexican government would come to its senses and seek a negotiated settlement.

Indeed, all military logic favored the United States. Mexico had no factories that produced modern rifles or cannons. Most Mexican soldiers marched with used rifles, bought from the British and last employed in the American Revolutionary War. Mexican artillery pieces also were outdated and unreliable. Moreover, the United States was a far larger country than its southern neighbor. In 1840, the American population stood at more than 17 million people. Mexico did not keep accurate census figures, but its population at the time was estimated at about 7 million.

The war was fought from 1846 to 1848. Today it bears scant mention in American history books largely because it was overshadowed by the great Civil War, which broke out thirteen years later. But in Mexico, the conflict remains a major event and a bitter memory. American historians call it the Mexican War or the Mexican-American War. Mexican historians also have two names for the conflict: the American Intervention in Mexico, and the American Invasion of Mexico.

CHAPTER 5

Warfare in Texas and Northern Mexico

The Mexican-American War was fought over an enormous land area on the North American continent. Basically it had three fronts: Texas and Northern Mexico, the Northern Frontier, and the Mexican Heartland. In Texas and Northern Mexico, the American forces were led by Zachary Taylor, a sixty-one-year-old officer originally from Virginia.

General Taylor was nicknamed "Old Rough and Ready" by his men. Rough he certainly was. Being overweight and sloppy in his dress, he did not look like a proper soldier, much less a general. Often he wore a scruffy pair of pants and donned the straw hat of a farmer. According to an often-told story, a lieutenant entered Taylor's camp one day seeking an audience with the general. He saw an old man cleaning a sword and assumed the man was General Taylor's servant. The lieutenant called him "Old Fatty," gave him his sword, and said he would like it cleaned; he offered a dollar for the cleaning services. Hours later, the lieutenant returned and was greeted by the same old man who was now wearing a cap with general's stars. The man said, in a commanding voice, "Lieutenant! I am General Taylor—and I will take that dollar."

Historians do not regard General Taylor as a brilliant army officer. He was slow to make up his mind, plodded when directing troop movements, and was overly cautious. But Taylor was well liked by his troops. He had years of combat experience, mostly in the Indian wars. When under fire, he was calm, steady, and fearless. His opponent in this early stage of the Mexican-American War was General Mariano Arista, forty-three years old and thought of as one of Mexico's most gifted officers.

An 1853 engraving of Mexican General Mariano Arista

On May 8, 1846, Taylor and Arista clashed at Palo Alto, a battlefield about five miles from the present-day city of Brownsville, Texas. Arista commanded 3,200 troops to Taylor's 2,300. The opening moves belonged to Arista. The Mexican general found Taylor's regiment and maneuvered his forces so they could quickly surround the Americans. Taylor ordered his men to advance, hoping to break the Mexican lines. Mexican cannons opened fire, but the big guns were of poor quality. Moreover, they shot solid cannonballs that fell short, bounced into the American ranks, and were relatively easy for the Yankees to dodge.

Early in the Battle of Palo Alto, sparks from cannons ignited the dry grass under the soldiers' feet. A brushfire broke out, covering both sides with smoke. This was the "fog of war," an unexpected event that often decides battles despite the careful plans of generals. Before the smoke blinded the soldiers, Arista ordered his men to attack to his right. Taylor saw the movement and repositioned his cannons to meet the enemy troops. When the advancing Mexicans broke out of the brush fire smoke, they expected to see enemy infantry. Instead they found themselves marching into the barrels of menacing-looking cannons. It was their first encounter with the *Yanquis'* secret weapon—"flying artillery."

Unknown to Mexican army officers, the Americans had developed new lightweight cannons that could be set up and dismantled quickly and moved by horse carriages. These new guns came to be called "flying artillery" because they were capable of swift movement from spot to spot. The concept of employing the fast-moving guns in battle was developed at West Point by Major Samuel Ringgold. By coincidence, Major Ringgold himself commanded the artillery units at the Battle of Palo Alto.

American guns opened up with exploding shells and with "grape shot," metal slugs that burst out of the muzzles in deadly shotgun-like blasts. Cannon fire ripped into Mexican ranks, cutting down the troops long before they got close enough to shoot their rifles or fight with bayonets. Above the roar of the cannons, wounded soldiers moaned and terrified horses screamed. A Mexican infantryman wrote, "[Our] soldiers died, not like victims in combat where they could kill as well as be killed . . . but in a fatal situation where they were helpless."

When the fighting finally wound down, the Mexican side had lost 230 men while the Americans had suffered nine dead. Ironically, one of the Americans killed was Major Ringgold. He saw his creation used for the first time in an actual battle, and the swift-moving guns clearly tipped the scale toward the American side.

Next came the grizzly task of cleaning up the battlefield. The dead lay strewn about, and corpses began to stink in the Texas heat after just a few hours. The smell of rotting flesh was a painful memory that would stay with the soldiers for the rest of their lives. The field of corpses attracted coyotes, wolves, and wild dogs. American Lieutenant E. Kirby Smith wrote that on all sides, "wolves [were] howling and fighting over their dreadful meal."

Two days later, on May 9, the armies fought again in a dry riverbed region called *Rescala de la Palma* (in Spanish, a dry river is a *rescala*). In this battle, General Arista himself led a charge of horse soldiers and infantrymen. Once more the attack was broken up by American artillery. General Artista was baffled. These cannons, the flying artillery, were so much different from Mexican big guns, which were emplaced at the beginning of a battle and never moved. Few Mexican soldiers actually took part in Arista's charge, but all saw their ranks ripped to pieces by American artillery. In the face of these menacing cannons, the soldiers panicked and ran. Many drowned trying to swim across the Rio Grande.

The battles of Palo Alto and Rescala de la Palma proved to be a foretaste of future clashes between the two warring armies. In most skirmishes, Mexicans on the battlefield outnumbered Americans. Mexican officers frequently ordered bayonet charges, because during close fighting with bayonets the side with greater numbers usually prevails. But American firepower—especially Yankee artillery—kept the Mexican troops at a safe distance from American ranks. This pattern would be repeated many times in the coming months. Mexican soldiers fought bravely, yet American superiority in weapons won the day.

After the battles, Zachary Taylor withdrew to Fort Texas, the earthen stockade that was constructed months earlier on the banks of the Rio Grande. The stockade was later named Fort Brown after Major Jacob Brown, who had been killed defending the fort during an early engagement. Later still, the border town of Brownsville, Texas, developed around the fort's walls.

Palo Alto Battlefield National Historic Site

The Battle of Palo Alto was fought on May 8, 1846, five days before America's official declaration of war on Mexico. It was one of the few engagements of the war that took place on what later became American soil. *Palo Alto* (Tall Timber) is named for a tree-covered ridge that rises above what was once a bloody battlefield. Today, the site is preserved as the Palo Alto Battlefield National Historic Park, which is located near Brownsville, Texas. Visitors at the park may follow the movements of troops once commanded by Zachary Taylor and Mariano Arista.

In Mexico City, people learned of the twin defeats at Palo Alto and Rescala de la Palma, and a heavy feeling of gloom hung over the capital. Everyone was shocked and asked the question: What happened to our army? Why did the men run? Some Mexicans came to believe that the *gringos* (Americans) were supermen who could not be defeated. A soldier who was present at the two battles added to this myth when he told a Mexico City newspaper that the Americans drank gunpowder mixed with whiskey for their morning meal. Still, most Mexicans were resolved to fight on. Said the governor of the state of Leon, "All Mexicans have felt pain and outrage [but one] loss does not lose the war. Mexico should fight to the end."

While men battled along the Rio Grande, intrigue ruled in the American capital. In 1846, a gentleman appeared in Washington seeking an audience with President Polk and claiming to be an agent for Antonio López de Santa Anna. He said Santa Anna wanted to conclude the war. If Santa Anna were allowed to return to Mexico,

Gringo

Gringo is a slang word used in Mexico to describe a white person, usually an American. Years ago, it was thought of as an offensive term, but today the word has lost its bite, and Americans living in Mexico commonly call each other *gringos*. There are two theories as to the origin of the word. One is that Mexicans, upon hearing a foreign language, will say, *"A mi es griego"* ("It's Greek to me"). The word *griego* can sound like *gringo*; hence, the word came into use. The second theory comes from the Mexican-American War. When Yankee troops hiked the roads of Mexico, they sang a marching song with the chorus "Green grow the lilacs." When the words *green grow* were heard from a distance by people who did not know the English language, they merged to become *gringo*.

the man said, he would assume the presidency and would sell California to the United States, thus ending the conflict. At the time, Santa Anna was in exile in Cuba and could not get to Mexican shores because the American navy blockaded all ports. Polk, who hoped for a quick end to the war, signed an order telling the navy to permit Santa Anna to return to Mexico.

Santa Anna landed in Veracruz in August 1846 and once more proved himself to be a turncoat. He immediately forgot the promises he had made to President Polk and told friends and followers he was now the "Savior of Mexico." The Savior then began raising an army and promising to defeat General Taylor and the despised *gringos*.

The exasperated Mexican people hoped and prayed for Santa Anna's success. They had no other choice. Many Mexicans disliked and certainly mistrusted Santa Anna, but no one else seemed capable of leadership at this crucial time. To the north, the American army stood poised to pour over the border, while at home Mexican politicians busied themselves with infighting. Liberals continued to fight with conservatives, and political splinter groups abounded. In 1846 alone, Mexico had four different presidents. Perhaps Santa Anna could achieve order and rally the army to victory. If he failed, the nation was lost.

Santa Anna named himself "acting president," but his primary focus was to lead the army in the field. This was where the action and the glory lie—in mortal combat against the *Yanquis*. The working president, who was little more than a puppet to Santa Anna's whims, was Gómez Farías. To Farías fell the unenviable job of raising money to supply the army. Farías turned to the one institution in Mexico that had ample funds: the Catholic Church. He implored the church to sell some of its vast property holdings to help fund the war effort. Catholic leaders were outraged and called government officials sinful for even requesting church money. Priests threatened to suspend Sunday services to the masses if the government continued its pressure. Pro-Catholic demonstrators took to the streets, and mobs threw rocks at the National Palace in Mexico City.

In May 1846, General Taylor moved a large force across the Rio Grande and occupied the city of Matamoros. This was the Americans' first venture into Mexico proper, and they took the city without firing a shot. Arista and his army had withdrawn to the south. Later, a board of inquiry dismissed General Arista because he had been so badly beaten in the two opening battles. Arista was one of the nation's most competent officers, but on him fell the shame of defeat. In fact, he was defeated by superior weapons more than superior generalship.

American soldiers in Matamoros were greeted by surprisingly friendly townspeople. The Rio Grande territory was far from the Mexican heartland, and local people felt mixed loyalties toward their remote national government. Americans bought food at the market from smiling street vendors. Oranges and bananas were rare in the north, but here market bins overflowed with the delicious fruits. Many Americans tasted chili peppers for the first time and found them to be fiery and exotic. Hot chocolate, a drink little known in the United States, was devoured by the troops. At night, the Yankees attended fandangos and did the lively dances with pretty Mexican girls. When the army first

American soldiers enjoyed the foods offered in
Matamoros that are still available in markets today.

entered Matamoros, General Taylor promised city officials that his men would behave in a responsible manner. For the most part, the regular troops did conduct themselves with dignity.

Then American volunteers came to the front.

At the time of the Mexican War, the American army numbered slightly more than 7,000 officers and men. Keeping a tiny standing army was national policy early in U.S. history. It was assumed that if the country were invaded, volunteer units would be raised by the various states and placed under regular army commanders. The notion of volunteer militias defending the United States dated back to the Minutemen and the War of Independence. In popular thinking, the volunteers were patriots and American heroes.

At the beginning of the war, President Polk asked for volunteers to serve in the struggle against Mexico. Patriotic fervor held sway in the United States, where many people were furious at the Mexicans because of the slaughter at the Alamo. Also, manifest destiny and the

African Americans and the American Military

Black men served honorably in U.S. conflicts before the Mexican War. African Americans also fought in the Civil War and in every one of their country's wars afterward. They did not, however, serve actively in the Mexican War. In the 1840s, strict rules barred African Americans from joining the military. Doctors were ordered to examine recruits and reject any man who they suspected had even a portion of black blood. A doctor's manual of the times said this policy was necessary because "soldiers would not tolerate the mixed breed as comrades." Some black slaves, usually owned by officers, accompanied their masters into the army and worked as their personal servants. Probably a handful of blacks managed to serve despite the restrictions, but for the most part the American army during the Mexican War was a whites-only establishment.

need to expand the borders to the Pacific was by this time a national passion.

In towns and cities around the nation, young men answered their country's call and signed commitments to serve as citizen soldiers for six to twelve months. Recruitment drives were accompanied by band music and politicians making speeches. Young ladies knitted flags for the volunteer militias to fly. In public ceremonies, the prettiest of the female knitters was assigned to make a speech and give the flag to the captain of a volunteer company while his men stood at attention behind him. One such speaker said, "We honor [the volunteers] for their patriotism, we respect them for their worth and virtue, we admire them for their beauty, and love them because we can't help it."

Appeals to patriotism and the fanfare of recruitment drives succeeded. During the Mexican War, more than 70,000 Americans served as volunteer soldiers. The regular army also expanded during the war years.

Most of the young men who joined the volunteers sincerely believed their country was in danger and it was their duty to come to its defense. Others, however, joined the units because they were unemployed, and still others because they were wanted by the law and faced a jail term. Some were adventurers who hungered to see a new land and wanted the army to pay for their trip.

In the field, the volunteer patriots as well as the potential bandits served together in the ranks. Discipline was a problem. Punishments for rule-breakers were meted out by company commanders who were themselves volunteers. In volunteer units, it was custom for the men to elect their officers. Many of the company commanders were aspiring politicians who dreamed of attaining high offices after the war. They needed the votes of men who now served under them, and they were reluctant to order severe punishments. Therefore, lawless volunteers often went free.

Trouble brewed when the volunteer units arrived in Mexico. Criminal types looked upon the Mexican civilian population—their goods as well as their women—as plunder, things to be taken as a soldier's right. A private in a regular unit complained in a letter to his father, "The majority of the Volunteers sent here are a disgrace to the nation; think of one of them shooting a woman while washing on the bank of the river—merely to test his rifle; another tore forcibly from a Mexican woman the rings from her ears. Their officers take no notice of these outrages, and the offenders escape."

The war was particularly popular in the western and southern states. In Tennessee, the call went out for 3,000 volunteers, and 30,000 flocked to sign up. Racism played a part in the American attitude toward the Mexican people. Most Mexicans were dark-skinned people and therefore were regarded with menace by many Americans from the southern and western portions of the country. (Remember that in the South, slavery was the rule; in the West, Indians were regarded as enemies.) One group of recently arrived volunteers from Arkansas shouted, "Show us the Mexican niggers."

Throughout history, war has bred hatred, and the Mexican War proved no exception to that pattern. Only a scant minority of Americans—volunteers as well as regulars—committed atrocities against the Mexican people, but the crimes perpetrated by the few burned in the Mexican memory for generations to come.

Early in 1846, Taylor's army occupied the city of Camargo, also near the Rio Grande. Camargo was normally a town of 2,000 people surrounded by pleasant fruit orchards. However, just weeks before Taylor's entrance, the town was struck by a devastating spring storm. Sudden heavy rains upset the region's ecology. Camargo became plagued in an almost biblical manner with snakes, scorpions, frogs, tarantulas, and biting ants. The rapid infestation bred killer diseases. Dysentery, fevers, and measles swept the American army. Volunteer units, which had especially poor sanitation practices, suffered the most. Men died by the hundreds.

Camargo was called the "Yawning Grave Yard." Buglers played the military death march so often that mockingbirds in the trees of Camargo learned to sing some of the notes.

The experience at Camargo was a harbinger for the grim fate that befell the American army during the Mexican War. Because of bad water and tropical diseases, far more American soldiers died of illness in Mexico than were killed on the battlefields.

In September 1846, the Mexican and American armies fought at the city of Monterrey in Northern Mexico. The Mexicans were led by General Pedro de Ampudia, a notoriously cruel commander who regularly executed his own men in order to enforce discipline. Ampudia once had fifteen rebellious soldiers shot. He then decapitated the rebels, boiled their heads in oil, and displayed the naked skulls in iron cages to warn others that he was the ultimate boss.

A hand-colored lithograph of the capture of Monterrey. The print appeared in a 1851 book titled *The War Between the United States and Mexico, Illustrated* by George Wilkins Kendall. Kendall commissioned German painter Carl Nebel, whom he had met in Mexico City, to create pictures that he then used to make prints to illustrate the book.

The Battle of Monterrey was a bloody house-by-house affair. In the maze of twisting streets and alleys, the Americans were unable to use their artillery in an effective manner. Once more, the Mexicans enjoyed numerical superiority: Ampudia commanded 10,000 troops to Taylor's 6,000. Mexican soldiers fought with particular courage, but Taylor organized an attack that came from two directions. Ampudia lacked the military skills to deploy his troops properly and take advantage of his greater numbers. Steadily, the Mexican defenders retreated. When the Mexicans were surrounded in the city plaza, Ampudia asked Taylor for a truce. Taylor agreed, and Ampudia and his soldiers were allowed to retreat from the city.

After the battle, a Mexican resident said, "Monterrey had become an enormous cemetery. The unburied bodies, the dead and rotting animals, the empty streets, everything gave the city a frightful appearance." Monterrey's suffering did not end when the fighting was over because troops of Texan volunteers moved into the city. The Texans had been battling Mexican forces for ten years, and hatred boiled in their ranks. An American named D. H. Hill reported, "Murder, rape, and robbery were committed by the [Texas] Volunteers in the broad light of day. . . . [They even] burnt the thatched huts of the miserable peasants."

President Polk fumed when he learned that General Taylor had allowed the Mexican troops to leave Monterrey after they surrendered. He claimed that Taylor had no authority to grant a truce to Ampudia and that he should have captured the entire

A lithograph of Mexican General Pedro de Ampudia surrendering to American General Zachary Taylor after the Battle of Monterrey in 1846.

Rebel Yell

Going into combat, Texans frequently yelled a high-pitched battle cry that was described as a "yee-ha" sound. A theory claims that they learned the war whoop from their enemies, the Comanches. It is also believed that the battle cry was picked up by volunteer units from southern states, and that it evolved into the famous "Rebel Yell." The Rebel Yell—a fearsome call to battle—was shrieked out by Confederate troops when they charged Yankee formations during Civil War clashes, such as those at Bull Run and Manassas.

army when he had the chance to do so. Polk told his cabinet that if Taylor had taken Ampudia's entire army prisoner, "[it] would probably have ended the war with Mexico."

Moreover, the president decried Taylor for his slowness in prosecuting the war. Polk knew that wars followed a certain pattern with the people at home. At first, wars tended to be well received, but if they dragged on the public lost enthusiasm for fighting. Already, Polk believed, the Mexican War had lasted too long. The American president had hoped the Mexicans would give up at first sight of the powerful American army, but instead the Mexicans continued their struggle. Moreover, the Battle of Monterrey indicated that their fighting qualities were improving.

To the south, Santa Anna raised an army that relied on a traditional Mexican method: rounding up impoverished men and forcing them at bayonet point to serve as soldiers. Morale in the army was dismal. Privates were often Indians who were denied civil rights and therefore had doubtful loyalties to their country. Army food was scarce and of poor quality. Desertion among enlisted men was common. Mexican weapons were always substandard. An American reporter said he saw "many [Mexican rifles] held together with leather straps." The army paid its expenses largely through "loans" (which were never repaid) extracted from rich people and from the very reluctant Catholic Church. The funds that were collected were often squandered by high-ranking officers, who purchased expensive horses and fancy uniforms for their own use.

In January 1847, Santa Anna led his army northward to meet General Taylor's forces. The march itself was an ordeal. Ill-trained and poorly fed, the men trekked across a waterless desert under a brutal sun. Fatigue alone killed many soldiers. While the men struggled on foot, their leader, Santa Anna, rode in a horse-drawn carriage that also carried cages of fighting cocks used for the amusement of his officer friends. Santa Anna began the march with 20,000 men, but he arrived in the Monterrey vicinity with about 15,000. The rest had either deserted, were too sick to walk, or had died along the road.

Still, Santa Anna believed he had a distinct advantage because his army outnumbered Taylor's by about three to one. Santa Anna halted his men at a gap in the mountains near a hacienda called Buena Vista. Confident of victory, he sent a note to General Taylor advising him to "surrender at discretion" because he faced certain slaughter. Old Rough and Ready delivered a letter to the Mexican general: "I beg leave to say I decline acceding to your request."

The Battle of Buena Vista, the biggest and bloodiest of the war, began. The battle proved that Mexican soldiers, though they were treated shabbily and had inferior equipment, were still willing to fight and die for their country.

The opening day of the battle, February 22, 1847, belonged to Santa Anna. The Mexican army attacked the Americans weak left flank, defended by a volunteer regiment from Indiana. The Indiana men were driven backward, and it seemed they would soon be routed.

General Taylor himself helped to rally the volunteers, and the American line held. At night, a dismal rain drenched troops on both sides. The Americans at least had some food to eat during this wretched night, but the Mexican soldiers went hungry.

The next morning, the Americans were greeted by a curious sight. In the foreground, Mexican infantry and the cavalry soldiers stood at attention while Catholic priests passed along their ranks blessing the men. Americans, since they practiced different faiths, did not mix religion with combat in this manner. Mexico was an entirely Catholic country in which priests preached the only accepted gospel. One American soldier claimed, "The air was clear and we could see every movement: The infantry knelt down, the Cavalry lowered their lances . . . as benedictions were bestowed."

An 1847 print of the Battle of Buena Vista, also known as the Battle of Angostura. An aide-de-camp of

Aside from its religious intent, the Catholic ceremony showed the Americans the large force they faced. It was, in effect, psychological warfare. The Yankees could not help but think that these thousands of troops, now blessed by God, would certainly overwhelm them.

With battle cries and cracks from rifles, fierce fighting broke out. Once more the opening stages went to the Mexicans. Taylor's men were mostly volunteers who lacked combat experience. The novice soldiers were stunned when they saw the Mexicans marching steadily toward them despite the deadly artillery fire raining down upon them. Shortly after the battle began, Major William Bliss rode up to General Taylor and told him the American troops had already been defeated. Taylor responded, "I know it, but the volunteers don't know it. Let them alone, we'll see what they do."

General Zachary Taylor created an on-the-spot sketch of the battleground, from which the print was made.

To Taylor's surprise, the volunteers' battle lines held and Santa Anna, who seemed to be at the threshold of an overwhelming victory, called off his attack. Taylor and the Americans did not know that Santa Anna had to return to Mexico City to put down still another military coup. Once more, political infighting damaged Mexico as much as the foreign army attacking from the north did.

In the capital, Santa Anna quickly defeated the rebellion, and he told his admirers he had achieved complete victory in the Battle of Buena Vista. He showed influential people several flags he had taken from

American volunteer companies and claimed the captured banners were symbols of his success.

In fact, the battlefield told a different story. It was true that Santa Anna had badly blooded Taylor's force; the Americans lost 267 men. But an estimated 1,500 Mexicans were also killed at Buena Vista. Most important, Santa Anna had failed to drive Taylor's army out of Northern Mexico, as was his intention. The Battle of Buena Vista was another failure in Mexico's war effort against the United States, as evidenced by the suffering of the wounded. Santa Anna left some eight hundred badly wounded men on the sands at Buena Vista. Historian Ramón Alcaraz wrote, "[They were] steeped in their blood, shivering with cold, parched with thirst, without shelter [and] saw their companions disappear. In sight already were the jackals and the dogs who awaited their frightful banquet."

Despite General Taylor's success against the Mexicans, President Polk recalled him after the Battle of Buena Vista. The president continued to blame Taylor's lack of military aggression for the nation's slow progress in winning the war. Politics also played a role in Taylor's dismissal. Taylor was a member of the Whig Party, which opposed Polk's Democratic Party. The popular general was being mentioned as a presidential candidate. In the eyes of the people, General Zachary Taylor, who had never lost a battle, was a genuine American hero.

President Taylor

In 1848, Taylor ran for president and won his country's highest office. On Inauguration Day, he succeeded James Polk, the man who had fired him a year earlier. Once he entered office, Taylor's health declined. He died in the White House on July 9, 1850, after serving as president for sixteen months.

Polk regarded Taylor's ever-increasing fame to be a political threat to him and his party.

The warfare in Northern Mexico fit a pattern that would hold true for the entire Mexican-American War. Mexican soldiers fought bravely, but they were overwhelmed by the superior weapons and military organization of the American army. Also, the Mexican government was in a constant state of chaos throughout the war years. It was as if Mexico fought two wars—one against the invading Americans and another against itself.

In this hand-colored woodcut of a nineteenth-century illustration, General Stephen Kearny captures the New Mexico territory from Mexico in 1846.

CHAPTER 6

The Occupation of the Northern Frontier

While the fighting raged in Northern Mexico, the American army turned its attention to the territory the nation coveted from the beginning: Mexico's Northern Frontier. Rarely did Polk say in public that acquiring this land was his primary war aim, but insiders knew the president's intentions. On May 30, 1846, Polk wrote in his diary, "I declared it my purpose to be to acquire, for the United States, California, New Mexico, and perhaps some others of the Northern Provinces of Mexico whenever a peace was made."

The coveted land was seemingly there for the taking. Mexico had no large armies north of the Rio Grande. Initially, at least, American forces simply moved onto the vast northern territories and occupied them rather than fighting for the regions in battles.

Lying to the west of Texas was New Mexico, the oldest and most populated region of the Northern Frontier. The Hispanic residents there came from families who had lived in New Mexico for more than one hundred years. Few family members had ever traveled to the Mexican heartland. In fact, New Mexicans had greater contact with the United States than they did with Mexico City.

Trade developed between New Mexico and the American state of Missouri with the opening of the Santa Fe Trail in 1821. The Santa Fe Trail ran 780 miles north and south and linked Santa Fe with Independence, Missouri. Every year, an average of eighty wagons lugged goods over this rocky path through the wilderness. Commerce on the road generated $1 million in sales annually. The city of Santa Fe became a commercial crossroad because it marked the northern end of the *Camino Real* (Royal Road), which led from the Mexican heartland to the Northern Frontier and the southern end of the Santa Fe Trail. The arrival of American wagon caravans always brought a wave of excitement to the village people in New Mexico. Upon seeing the wagons, New Mexicans shouted, *"Viene los Americanos!"* ("Here come the Americans!"). Everyone rushed to the roadside to behold the latest products from the land of the Yankees.

Trail of Yore

The Santa Fe Trail was first used in 1821 by William Becknell, a Missouri merchant who made a fortune trading American items such as ink, oil lamps, and medicines to New Mexicans for gold, furs, and horses. The trail was difficult and dangerous. Travelers often had to fight Indian warriors who tried to run off with goods and livestock. Shortly after it opened, the trail became a two-way street as New Mexican trading parties began going north, taking products to Missouri. A favorite trade item from New Mexico was the mule, a tough and strong farm animal. The Missouri Mule (which originally came from New Mexico) was widely used in that American state, and it is now Missouri's state animal. Over the years, the Santa Fe Trail grew to become a storied part of American western lore. Poems, novels, and movies were written that celebrated the adventure and romance of the Santa Fe Trail.

In August 1846, excitement gripped New Mexico because once more the *gringos* were moving down the Santa Fe Trail. But this time the men were not traders. They were instead soldiers, and Santa Fe residents feared they intended to plunder and burn Santa Fe, the New Mexican capital. New Mexico's priests added to the tension when they warned the people that the American troops would commit a host of crimes—rape, robbery, and murder. Worst of all, according to the priests, the *gringos* would nail the church doors shut and ban the Catholic religion.

The governor of New Mexico was a notoriously corrupt politician named Manuel Armijo. Months earlier, he had vowed to gather an army and fight the American invaders. But now that they were at the city's gates, the governor fled south. He took flight only after looting the city treasury of a fortune in gold and silver coins. Escaping with Governor Armijo were the best troops in New Mexico's militia, leaving the people of Santa Fe to await their grim fate with no protection at all.

Into the city came an American army regiment of 1,700 officers and men. They did not parade through the streets like triumphant warriors. Instead they straggled in looking weary, their uniforms in rags. The Americans had marched more than eight hundred miles down the Santa Fe Trail. The countryside was hotter and dryer than usual, and the men were exhausted.

The Americans were led by General Stephen Watts Kearny, who had been born in New Jersey to a wealthy family. He joined the army as a young man and was assigned to the wild and unexplored West. Kearny fell in love with the land. With almost religious zeal, he blazed trails and thrilled in the discoveries he encountered behind each new mountain. One of his greatest adventures came in 1819 when he led a small band of soldiers on an exploration mission of the Yellowstone River. Few whites had seen the Yellowstone Valley before Kearny. Given his experience in the wilds, Kearny was the perfect choice to head what was called the Army of the West. This special army was given the task of seizing Mexico's Northern Frontier, much of which was comprised of unexplored land.

Upon entering Santa Fe, Kearny's men behaved in a civil manner. The general was a strict disciplinarian and told his soldiers he would not tolerate abuse of the New Mexican people. He wanted the cooperation and the friendship of the locals. After just a few days, the men and women of Santa Fe relaxed, believing these *Americanos* meant them no harm. In a ceremony at the city plaza, Kearny assembled the citizens and made a speech: "I, Stephen W. Kearny, General of the Army of the United States, have taken possession of the province of New Mexico . . . . I am your governor—look to me for protection."

At the conclusion of the speech, the American flag was run up the flagpole and Kearny's soldiers cheered. It marked the first time in history that an American army had captured a foreign capital.

The Palace of the Governors

General Kearny made his speech in front of Santa Fe's historic Palace of the Governors. The low-slung adobe structure had been constructed by Spaniards in the year 1600, and it is recognized as the oldest continually used public building in the United States. Now a history museum, Santa Fe's Palace of the Governors holds some 800,000 items pertaining to the colorful past of the American Southwest.

General Kearny reached out to the people of Santa Fe and the surrounding towns, telling them the benefits they could expect under the government of the United States. Most important, Kearny offered protection. New Mexico was made up of Hispanic settlements and Pueblo Indian farm communities. All rural New Mexican villages suffered from raids by the nomadic Indians tribes, especially the Navajos. In one speech to New Mexico farmers, Kearny said, "From the Mexican government you have never received protection. The Apaches and Navajos come down from the mountains and carry off your sheep, and even your women, whenever they please. My government . . . will keep off the Indians."

Kearny and President Polk viewed New Mexico primarily as a path to the rich lands of California. Just weeks after his arrival in Santa Fe, General Kearny believed New Mexico was well established in the American fold and thus made plans to march west toward the Pacific. His conquest of New Mexico had been accomplished without firing a shot. Perhaps that conquest was too easy.

In September 1846, a confident Stephen Kearny split the Army of the West into three groups. One group remained in New Mexico to keep that territory secure. A second group was assigned to march south and join in an American effort to capture the Mexican city of Chihuahua. The general himself took a third unit west to California. Military historians point out that a commander who divides his army while in hostile territory will often regret his decision.

The Navajos observed Kearny taking the bulk of his forces out of the Santa Fe region. They believed the American soldiers were giving up their occupation of New Mexico and viewed the Yankee retreat as a chance to strike. Shouting war whoops, the Navajos stormed onto farms and ranches killing people and riding off with hundreds of sheep and horses. The series of raids were so lightning-quick that the American soldiers who had been left behind to secure Santa Fe were unable to intervene. The lesson was clear to New Mexicans: the *gringos* could not even keep their promise to protect them from Navajo raiders.

As the weeks went by, New Mexicans began looking upon the foreign troops patrolling their villages as an occupying army. Such armies of occupation are almost always detested. The conduct of the American soldiers helped fuel the bad feelings. Kearny's men were primarily volunteers from Missouri. They behaved properly when the stern general was in personal command, but when Kearny left on his march to California discipline in the ranks broke down. Soldiers indulged in fiery local wines. One New Mexican villager said of the Missouri volunteers, "A more drunken and depraved set I am sure can never be found."

Trouble began with an unlikely group of New Mexicans: the Pueblos. Normally, the Pueblo Indians were the most peace-loving people in New Mexico. Though they had long accepted Christianity, they still practiced many of their ancient religious rites when out of sight of the priests. Mostly they were interested in tending their farms and raising their families.

After Kearny left the region, several Pueblo leaders were arrested because American authorities suspected that they were plotting against the government. On a frosty night in January 1847, a group of Pueblo men banged on the door of the newly appointed American governor of New Mexico and demanded the release of their fellows. Governor Charles Bent, who had lived for many years in New Mexico, claimed that matter was up to the courts to decide. "We will [kill] you," the Pueblo leader roared, "and then we will kill every last American in New Mexico." Bent was shot down with arrows. Some reports claim he was scalped while still alive.

Insurrection broke out all over New Mexico as Pueblos allied with Hispanics attacked their American occupiers. The conflict often degenerated into a race war that pitted dark-skinned people against whites. Since the opening of the Santa Fe Trail, many American men had moved to New Mexico and married Hispanic and Indian women. Now those women smeared mud on the faces of their light-skinned children to protect them from the hate-crazed bands rampaging about and lashing out at everyone with white skin.

American soldiers stationed in Santa Fe rallied, shooting and capturing scores of rebels and driving the rest north to Taos Pueblo. After the fighting died down, both sides counted their losses. Dozens of Americans and about two hundred insurgents had been killed. Many Pueblos and Hispanics who had participated in the rebellion were thrown into jail.

After a quick trial, six of the prisoners—all of them Pueblos—were condemned to be hanged. The execution was carried out at Taos Pueblo on a foggy morning in April 1847. The condemned men were placed on a mule-driven wagon and taken to a huge tree, where six nooses were tied to a limb. During the wagon ride, several prisoners cursed Americans with what proved to be their last words. At the tree, they were told to stand. Nooses were placed around their necks, and a driver ordered the mules forward, causing the men to fall off the wagon and die by hanging. According to an American observer, "Two of the Pueblos managed to clasp hands [and the handshake] held till the muscles loosened in death."

The second group of Kearny's forces headed south under the command of Colonel Alexander William Doniphan. Colonel Doniphan was a red-haired man who stood well over six feet tall and was a successful trial lawyer in Missouri. His destination was the city of Chihuahua, which lies some three hundred miles below the Rio Grande. While still north of the river, Doniphan's regiment crossed a stretch of desert called by Spaniards *La Jornada del Muerto* (The Journey of the Dead). The name was appropriate. It was a forlorn, waterless trail lined with the sun-dried bones of horses and mules and the remains of broken wagons—mute witnesses to the deadly nature of this path. Finally, the exhausted Americans reached a clearing called *Brazito* (Little Arm), so named because it stood on a curving branch of the Rio Grande. Colonel Doniphan relaxed and started a card game with his fellow officers. Scouts suddenly raced up to the game with news that a Mexican army was approaching. Doniphan cursed because he held what he believed to be a winning hand and now had to quit the game and fight a battle.

Colonel Alexander William Doniphan

The Mexican force was led by a major with a famous name: Ponce de León. In the early 1500s, the major's distant Spanish relative had explored much of Florida while searching for the storied Fountain of Youth. Major Ponce de León was, like many other Mexican officers, an aristocrat who obtained his command not because of his military skills but through his influence in government circles. The Americans were better armed than his men. Also, in one of the few such cases in the Mexican-American War, the Americans under Doniphan outnumbered his Mexican force. Despite these daunting odds, Ponce de León ordered his men to charge.

The Battle of El Brazito took place on Christmas Day, 1846. It was a slaughter. In a firefight that lasted perhaps forty minutes, everything that could go wrong went wrong for the Mexicans. When Ponce de León ordered his bugler to play charge, he played retreat instead. Confusion reigned in the Mexican ranks. At the end of the battle, an American reported, "The field was strewn with bodies of men and horses." All the dead were soldiers of Ponce de León. As many as one hundred Mexicans were killed or wounded while the Americans suffered seven wounded and none killed.

On December 27, Doniphan occupied the city of El Paso. This village of traders and merchants generally welcomed the foreign army. The Missouri men found El Paso to be a pleasant town. One of the Americans, John Hughes, said they enjoyed "visiting and conversing with the fair señoritas of the place whose charms . . . almost induced some of the men to wish not to return home." El Paso was also a wine-making center, and many Missouri volunteers drank themselves into a stupor and suffered hangovers as a result.

After resting in El Paso, Colonel Doniphan led his regiment south toward the city of Chihuahua. It was a brutal trek over land that reminded the men of their previous march through the territory called The Journey of the Dead. This region of Northern Mexico was dry and virtually treeless. The sands under the men's feet swarmed with rattlesnakes and tarantulas. Traveling with Doniphan was a large party of American traders, who had joined the Missourians in El Paso. The traders formed a wagon train of more than three hundred mule-drawn vehicles in various states of repair. The squealing of wheels and clanging of pots and pans inside the wagons made a racket that could be heard for miles.

Defending Chihuahua was Mexican General García Conde, a clever officer who had studied previous battles with the *Yanquis* and determined that recklessly charging into their artillery was a disastrous mistake. So, García Conde decided to fight a defensive battle. He ordered his men to dig fortifications along the Sacramento River some fifteen miles north of town. It was a sound, orthodox plan that prob-ably would have worked against an orthodox enemy commander. But Doniphan was no orthodox commander. In fact, he was not a regular army officer at all, and many of his military moves defied conventions.

General García Conde built his fortified positions in front of the main road, a logical approach for any foe wanting to enter Chihua-hua. The Mexican general was so confident of victory that he loaded a wagon with ropes that he intended to use to tie the Missourians to their saddles after he took them prisoner. Doniphan scouted ahead and observed the fortifications. Rather than devising a way to attack the positions, he searched for a place to circumvent them.

The Missouri colonel determined that the desert land off the road to the left was hard enough to support his artillery pieces, and he sim-ply marched around the Mexican defenders. Once on the Mexican flank, he turned his artillery and gave the command to open fire. The Mexican troops were inexperienced to the point where most of them had never heard the sounds of cannons before. Belching fire and smoke, the great cannon roars seemed to them like thunder ringing out from the depths of hell. The troops panicked and ran. The Americans se-cured another easy victory at the Battle of the Sacramento River on February 28, 1847.

On March 1, Doniphan entered Chihuahua. He hoped to win the hearts of the citizens by entertaining them, and he ordered the regi-mental band to parade down the main street while playing "Yankee Doodle." The townspeople watched the parade in icy silence. Chihua-hua was the deepest penetration of Mexico yet made by the Army of the West. People there had stronger attachments to the national gov-ernment, and their resentment of the Yankee invaders was evident.

The pattern of Colonel Doniphan's advance and Mexican resistance was repeated again and again in the Mexican-American War. Both sides faced grave challenges. The Americans often had to march long distances over deserts and mountains even before they arrived at their objective, and then had to fight. Long treks to battlefields proved to be as arduous and as dangerous as was combat with the foe. The Mexican army, on the other hand, was simply not a match for a modern military organization. Individually, Mexican troops fought with courage. However, their army units were accustomed to putting down rebellious citizens in the country's almost never-ending civil wars. Mexican soldiers knew how to fight each other, but they were overwhelmed when facing a well-equipped modern army from a foreign nation.

General Stephen Kearny

One American officer who had to overcome the challenge of distance was General Stephen Kearny. His goal was California, almost a half a continent to the west.

Eleven days after he left Santa Fe, Kearny and his troop of about three hundred Missourians camped at the village of Socorro in New Mexico. In the distance, they saw a dust cloud and heard the rumble of horses' hoofs. All the Americans reached for their rifles. This was either an Indian raid or an attack by the Mexican cavalry. When the riders got closer, they could see that some were Indians but others were Americans. Kearny's men cheered and threw hats in the air. In this hostile land of New Mexico, they had chanced upon their own forces.

The leader of the horsemen dismounted and introduced himself to Kearny. He was Christopher "Kit" Carson, who had already won national fame as an adventurer and explorer. Carson had been born in Kentucky and grown up in Missouri. As a young man, he had traveled to the untamed West to make his living as a trapper, or what

The Mountain Men

Mountain men were true rugged individuals. They worked independently as fur trappers in the Rocky Mountain region. About 3,000 of them toiled in the fur trade from the 1820s to the 1840s. While searching the wilderness for fur-bearing animals, the mountain men trekked over territory previously seen only by Native Americans. One notable mountain man was James Beckwourth, a black man who had been born into slavery. Beckwourth discovered the Beckwourth Pass through the Sierra Mountains, which was later used by Americans traveling to California. Because of their raw courage and their adventurous spirit, the mountain men became legends in American history.

Americans called a "mountain man." Newspaper stories and entire novels had been written about Kit Carson, who was hailed as a fearless Indian fighter and a bold blazer of new trails in the western wilderness.

Carson brought exciting news: Americans already occupied California. The American army colonel John C. Frémont, who had been on a scouting mission, built a fort near Monterrey and pronounced that the territory was now a possession of the United States. Also, American frontiersmen and sailors, acting on their own, had raised a flag with a picture of a grizzly bear on its face over an outpost in northern California. That act was later called the Bear Flag Revolt, and the flag-raisers claimed they were taking California away from Mexico and founding a new country.

Believing California was securely in American hands, Kearny sent two hundred of his troops back to Santa Fe and pressed westward with about a hundred followers. One of the men remaining with Kearny was Kit Carson. No other American knew the western wilderness as well as he, and Kearny's men felt confident that their march to California would be successful with Carson as their guide. But all knew that they shouldn't anger Carson. Though a small man, he was possessed of a fiery temper and was quick to gun down anyone who he believed had wronged him.

The vastly reduced Army of the West marched west over desert land in what are now the states of New Mexico and Arizona. Kearny called it "a rough and barren country." He added, "It surprised me to see so much land that can never be of any use to man or beast. We traveled many days without seeing a spear of grass."

In early December 1846, Kearny approached San Pascual, a tiny village just east of San Diego, California. The small army had just crossed what is now the western half of the United States and completed one of the longest marches in American military history. Its mules and horses were exhausted. A torrential rain had fallen the previous two days, rendering rifles and powder useless. Worst of all, near San Pascual, Kearny learned that the *Californios* (the Mexican people

The Bear Flag Revolt

On June 14, 1846, a group of American residents raised the Bear Flag over Sonoma, California, a settlement just north of present-day San Francisco. The Americans proclaimed they had established a new country, the California Republic. The flag itself was made by a settler named William L. Todd, who was a first cousin to Mary Todd Lincoln, the wife of the future president. The California Republic lasted only twenty-six days before the entire California region was annexed by the United States. The original homemade flag boasting the picture of a grizzly was destroyed in a fire started by the great San Francisco earthquake of 1906.

of California) had revolted against American soldiers and had retaken their settlements. Kearny would now be forced to fight for California, and his men and animals were clearly in no condition for combat.

As was true with much of the Northern Frontier, California was an isolated region whose people felt only loose ties with the Mexican central government. Travel to California was so difficult that only about 5,000 Mexicans lived there at the time Kearny arrived. Americans were no strangers to the region because for years Yankee ships had called at ports such as San Diego, Monterrey, and San Francisco (then called Yerba Buena).

Kearny saw a militia unit of *Californios* mounted on their horses on the trail ahead of his army. At first he was surprised to discover that these men were old-fashioned lancers. They were armed with spears about nine feet long with small flags tied near the points (the flags were placed there to confuse enemy horses). In the distance the *Californios* looked, almost comically, like the medieval horse soldiers who had fought wars for the king of England.

Expecting an easy victory, Kearny separated his men into columns and ordered an attack. This time, from the beginning, everything went wrong for the Americans. A lieutenant at the head of the column was told to advance his men at a trot, but the officer thought he had heard the order to race forward at a full gallop. The leading group of Americans plunged unsupported into the *Californio* lancers, who jabbed at them with their spears. The fighting was so bloody that it shocked even veteran soldiers. Kearny discovered that the *Californio* lancers were superb horsemen. They communicated silently with their mounts, using their spurs to tell the horses when to turn and bank while all the time concentrating on thrusting their spears into enemy soldiers. Kearny later wrote, "They [the Californios] are the very best riders in the world. There is hardly one not fit for the circus."

Kearny's men did not have the advantage of firepower, as the recent torrential rains soaked their gunpowder and rendered their rifles useless. They fought using rifles as clubs, and they were quickly overwhelmed by the lancers and their skilled employment of spears.

In the first fifteen minutes of fighting, more than twenty Americans were killed and dozens more wounded. Kearny himself suffered spear wounds in the lower back and on his arm. Kit Carson was thrown off his horse. The ground below the battling horsemen became soaked in blood.

This action, the Battle of San Pascual, was fought near San Diego on December 6 and 7, 1846. It was one of the few battles in the Mexican-American War that the Americans lost. But the *Californios* never had the strength to chase the Americans out

Kit Carson

of California. Kearny recovered from his wounds and pushed on to San Diego. In that city, he met American naval forces under the command of Commodore Robert Stockton, and the two officers eventually consolidated the Pacific region for the United States. Stephen Kearny became military governor of California.

With California in the fold, President Polk achieved his primary war aim. However, the conflict continued because the Mexicans, though appearing to be beaten, simply would not quit.

An 1890 theatrical poster depicting the twenty-day
siege of the key Mexican seaport of Veracruz

CHAPTER 7

War in the Mexican Heartland

By early 1847, Americans at home had grown war-weary. The Mexican War, which many believed would be over in a matter of months, now approached its first year. Casualty lists grew longer. Far more American soldiers died of diseases in Mexico than in battle, but the letters home announcing wartime deaths shattered families as such letters do in all wars. Political opponents blamed the president for the prolonged conflict, which they derisively called "Mr. Polk's War." Polk, a Southerner and a slaveholder, never escaped the charge that he entered the war in order to extend the system of slavery into Mexico's Northern Frontier territory and even into Mexico itself.

From the beginning, the president hoped to win quickly in Mexico, gain the Northern Frontier, and then get out. Polk expected that the Mexican government would seek a settlement after just one or two defeats at the hands of the powerful United States Army. When this did not happen, Polk blamed General Taylor for not properly punishing the Mexicans on the battlefield and thereby forcing them to the peace table. The American chief sought a new military leader in General Winfield Scott.

If General Taylor was true to his nickname, "Old Rough and Ready," then Winfield Scott was also true to his: "Old Fuss and Feathers." He acquired the name because he was fond of brightly colored uniforms and was meticulous in his dress. He even entered combat perfectly groomed and looking as if he were about to step upon the parade ground. Above all, Winfield Scott was a fighting general. When fighting the British during the War of 1812, Scott was severely wounded and had two horses shot from underneath him. Still, he refused to leave the battlefield and had to be carried off.

General Winfield Scott

Scott was given the incredible task of landing from the sea at Veracruz and then marching to the Mexican heartland. This invasion was a move President Polk hoped he would never have to make, but the Mexicans proved to be stubborn foes. Grimly, the president accepted that it would take the occupation of Mexico City to bring a close to this war.

Veracruz was an amphibious landing requiring cooperation between the army and navy. The American navy assembled a fleet of two hundred ships of various types. This flotilla approached the Mexican coast in March 1847. The port city of Veracruz was protected by a triangular-shaped fort with high stone walls. The fortress, called San Juan de Ullúa, was one of the strongest such redoubts found anywhere in the Americas.

Scott ordered the Veracruz commander to surrender while promising safe passage for civilians. The Mexican commander refused to even respond to his request. With roars sounding like thunder from the sea, the American fleet opened fire. For three days, warships pounded Veracruz with their cannons. Naval shells battered the walls of the fort, and they also fell among helpless civilians in the city. A Mexican reporter in the city wrote, "How horrible is the scene . . . women and children [are] perishing from the effects of the explosions, or under the ruins of their dwellings . . . the streets [are covered] with their blood."

Three miles south of the city, out of range of the fort's cannons, ships crowded with soldiers edged close to the beach. Troops disembarked and began the long and difficult task of unloading heavy artillery pieces and dragging them through the sands toward harder grounds inland. The American cannons quickly became mired in the mud near shore. This, of course, would be the perfect time to attack the Americans and drive them back into the sea, but the bulk of Mexican forces were busy elsewhere. Antonio López de Santa Anna, the army chief, was in Mexico City fighting rival officers who were plotting an overthrow of his government.

In Veracruz, the Americans continued their artillery attack, slaughtering soldiers and civilians alike. At eight in the morning on March 26, 1847, a squad of Mexican troops led by an officer carrying a white flag marched out of the fort. Firing ceased as Mexican and American officers converged outside the city walls to discuss terms. Veracruz, at last, surrendered to the Americans.

The city by this time lay in shambles. During the siege, American cannons had poured more than 7,000 rounds into Veracruz. Houses, churches, and buildings of all kinds crumbled to dust under the bombardment. Some eight hundred city dwellers were killed and many times that number were injured. An American volunteer wrote home, "I cannot relate to you all [that I have seen in Veracruz]; my heart sickens in the attempt, what a horrible thing is war."

The amphibious landing of the American forces under General Scott at Veracruz, as depicted by American lithographer Nathaniel Currier

Serving under Scott was a captain from Virginia, Robert E. Lee, who would years later lead Confederate forces against the North in the American Civil War. Lee gazed at the ruins of Veracruz and wrote to his wife, "My heart bled for the inhabitants."

Veracruz served as the entry point for General Scott's march to Mexico City. Scott decided to approach the capital over the National Road. This was an ancient passage once used by the Aztecs and taken by the Spaniard Hernán Cortés in his trek inland. The roadway ran more than two hundred miles over mountains and deserts. Scott and all the Americans knew that Santa Anna and his army were bound to put up a fight somewhere along the way. Facing these challenges, General Scott ordered his army of 10,000 troops to advance toward Mexico City in early April 1847.

Veracruz—Viva la Fiesta!

Veracruz today is known as a party town, a place given over to fiestas with wild music and dancing. Its great fiesta, *Carnival*, celebrated before Lent, is world famous. The city's restaurants, many of which specialize in serving delicious seafood, are considered among the best in Mexico. Each day, hundreds of tourists visit the waterfront fort of San Juan de Ullúa. This fortress, first built in the 1580s, was designed to protect the city from pirates. It later served as a very grim prison, and in 1847 it became the first step in the American conquest of Mexico.

Boulevard Manuel Avila Camacho during Carnival

News of the defeat at Veracruz and the suffering of the civilians there reached Mexico City. Panic gripped the capital as the people feared for the day when the hated *Yanquis* would storm onto the streets. The Americans were said to be godless monsters who wantonly killed women and children and blew up churches. Once more the Mexicans looked to Santa Anna as their only hope. Masses cheered as he rode in his carriage from one office to another. All knew that Antonio López de Santa Anna was as changeable as the winds and as slippery as the rain. But he was all Mexico had, the only hope of the *patria*, the fatherland. Before he left to defend the capital, Santa Anna told a gathering, "My duty is to sacrifice myself. . . . I [intend] to die fighting."

Santa Anna reorganized his army as he prepared to meet Scott. New soldiers were drafted and drummed into the ranks. Life for the common soldier was one of hardships, poor food, virtually no pay, and the constant fear of brutal punishments imposed by officers.

The Mexican army reflected Mexican society. Foot soldiers came from the poor or peasant classes. As was the case with average peasants, enlisted men were denied basic rights and treated harshly by superiors. Officers, on the other hand, were pampered and lived in relative comfort. They came from the upper or land-owning classes and were thought of as gentlemen. Life in Mexico was cruelly unequal, and the army mirrored the conditions of the country at large.

Yet Mexican common soldiers enjoyed entertainment, most of which was entirely their own creation. Music, which included singing and guitar playing, abounded in their camps. The men gambled with dice and cards, played sports, and drank cactus beer (*pulque*), usually to excess. Their camps mimicked life in the villages, where people used parties to enjoy stolen moments of joy. Village peasants hated and mistrusted government leaders; army soldiers regarded officers as their enemies. Therefore, drinking and singing with friends—all of whom were comrades and members of the same social class—served as a vital release, an escape for an otherwise gloomy routine.

Mexican infantrymen had one benefit that their American counterparts only dreamed about: the companionship of women. The Mexican ranks were made up of male soldiers (*soldaderos*) and female soldiers (*soldaderas*). Officially, the *soldaderas* were not recognized as members of the military. Instead, they were common-law wives and girlfriends who lived and marched with the troops. They were, however, not mere camp followers. Most were attached to just one soldier and served as that man's mistress, laundress, cook, and nurse. Most soldiers would have married their companion *soldaderas*, but marriage in Mexico was an expensive undertaking. To become married required payments to the government for a license and money to the church for its blessings. Officers got married; foot soldiers did not. *Soldaderas* had a long history with the Mexican army, and they were not afraid to fight. When her man fell, a *soldadera* commonly picked up his rifle and took his place on the battlefield. Stories, poems, and folk songs were written hailing the courage of Mexican *soldaderas*.

The army's chief, Santa Anna, took great pride in his ability as a tactician. He was excellent at judging a battlefield—observing the lay of the land and determining where to make a stand when fighting a defensive battle and where to attack when on the offensive. However, he had a glaring weakness: he did not appreciate the conditions facing his men. Santa Anna arrived on a battlefield and deployed his regiments without knowing or perhaps without caring if the soldiers in the ranks were tired after a long march or hungry after going days without food. He often called his troops his "little chickens," and he expected them to fight despite their hunger or fatigue.

Santa Anna lived in the Veracruz region and knew that the dreaded disease yellow fever was ever-present there. He took great pains to draft soldiers from Veracruz or other coastal areas because they had some immunity to the sickness. Yellow fever had defeated foreign invaders in the past, and Santa Anna hoped it would again work its evil against the Americans. The Mexican general built a defensive position at a mountain pass along the National Road called *Cerro Gordo* (Fat Hill). East of Cerro Gordo lay the coastal plains, where yellow fever prevailed; to the west rose the mountains that were free of the sickness. Santa Anna believed if he could pin the Americans in the fever-ridden coastal lands, their soldiers would sicken and the army would be forced to withdraw.

Yellow Fever, Curse of the Coast

Yellow fever, which causes severe illness and often death, most likely originated in Africa and was spread by the slave trade. Years ago, it affected coastal regions in many parts of the Americas. Its symptoms included a yellowing of the skin—hence the name. The disease is carried from person to person by mosquitoes that inhabit seacoasts. Those mosquitoes are less prevalent in the mountains. Today, yellow fever is controlled by vaccination.

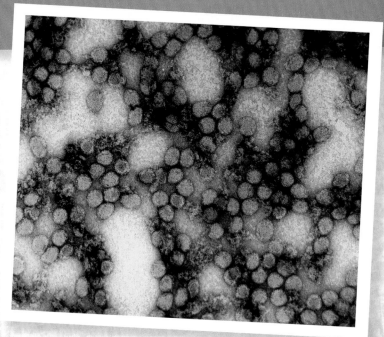

In mid-April 1847, Scott's forces approached Cerro Gordo, which lay about sixty miles inland and some ten miles east of Jalapa. The town of Jalapa was considered to be the gateway to the fever-free mountainous regions of central Mexico. Cerro Gordo itself was a natural fortress where the National Road was flanked between two steep hills. Santa Anna commanded 12,000 men at Cerro Gordo, and he positioned them in trench lines along the hills. Confidently, he awaited Scott's army of about 8,000 Americans.

Winfield Scott was a scientific officer who explored all approaches to a battlefield before launching an attack. He sent a patrol of engineers ahead on the National Road to determine the best route for his advance. Heading that engineer unit was Captain Robert E. Lee. Under the cover of darkness, Lee discovered a rocky hill that Santa Anna had failed to fortify. Working through the night, Lee and his men pushed cannons up to the hilltop. When the sun rose in the morning, the Mexicans on the opposite side of the National Road found the muzzles of those cannons pointing down at them. In the Mexican-American War, Robert E. Lee displayed the brilliance he would later show as the most effective commander on either side of the American Civil War.

The Battle of Cerro Gordo was fought on April 17 and April 18, 1847. Once more it was one-sided—a bitter defeat for Santa Anna and the Mexican army. After a booming artillery duel, Scott ordered his men to charge Cerro Gordo with their bayonets. An American soldier, seeing combat for the first time, was stunned by the ferocity of the fighting: "It seemed like murder to see men running bayonets into each other's breasts."

American lithographer Richard Magee depicts the flight of Santa Anna at the Battle of Cerro Gordo in this print (circa 1847).

Many hundreds of Mexican soldiers were killed and wounded at Cerro Gordo. About 3,000 Mexicans, including more than two hundred officers and even five generals, surrendered. Santa Anna managed to escape on horseback, but his carriage was captured by a unit of Illinois volunteers. In the carriage, the Illinois men found a prize of war: one of Santa Anna's wooden legs. They sent the peg leg home, where it would be displayed for many years at the Illinois State Capitol building. The artificial limb is today kept at an Illinois National Guard history museum in Springfield, Illinois.

As usual, cleanup after the battle was a grizzly task. Mexican prisoners worked with American troops to dig mass graves and drag corpses into them. The ground was covered with twisted and mangled bodies, almost all of them Mexicans. A newspaperman from the United States reported that "they lay thick around, and a more horrible scene it would be difficult to picture. Mexicans lay dead in every direction; some resting against trees, others with legs and arms extended." Americans were shocked to see the large number of women, the *soldaderas*, who were killed alongside their men. Everyone expected to see dead men on a battlefield, but so many female bodies surprised and numbed the senses of Yankee soldiers.

Cerro Gordo opened the gates for Scott's march to Mexico City. For Mexicans, it was the most dispiriting defeat of the war. José Fernando Ramírez, a congressman from Mexico City, claimed that Cerro Gordo was "a route as complete as it was shameful. Everything was lost. Absolutely nothing was saved, not even hope."

Once again, this latest lost battle convinced many Mexicans that the *Yanquis* were supermen and to try to defeat them in battle was futile. Congressman Ramírez wrote:

> The troops have come back [from Cerro Gordo] much depressed. The leaders and officers declare that the Yankees are invincible and the soldiers are telling terrible tales that bring to mind the [Spanish] Conquest. Some say the enemy soldiers are such huge, strong men that they can cut an

opponent in two with a single swipe of their swords. It is also said their horses are gigantic and very fast. . . . Let us say nothing about their artillery, which has inspired fear and terror in all our troops.

Unknown to the Mexicans, Scott was having troubles of his own. The war had lasted too long. Thousands of volunteers had signed up for a twelve-month commitment, and those terms were close to expiring. Scott asked the volunteers to extend their service time, but few opted to do so. Scott had no choice but to let the volunteers go home. Therefore, he was forced to watch his ranks diminish. Also, the American units were being hit with a rash of desertions. Men wandered off from their companies and tried to get home on their own, or they decided to live in Mexico. A few deserters did the ultimate turncoat act and joined the Mexican army. The Mexicans encouraged the American turncoats by offering them high pay and land grants in Mexico after the war.

At Puebla, the second-largest city in Mexico, General Scott rested his men. Many officers who were knowledgeable about history commented that some three centuries earlier the Spaniard Hernán Cortés had also made a prolonged stop at Puebla before proceeding on to Mexico City. The parallels between Scott and Cortés were many. Both commanded small armies compared to their opposition. Both were foreigners invading the heartland of a huge country. Cortés was successful largely because of infighting among the Mexicans. The dominant tribe, the Aztecs, was hated by rival tribes, and the Mexican people could not unite to repel a foreign enemy. Now, similar infighting weakened Mexican society and, once again, made the nation vulnerable to foreign conquest.

While in Puebla, Scott hosted an important visitor: diplomat Nicholas Trist. Trist had been appointed by President Polk to open negotiations with Mexico with the aim of ending the war. It would seem that Trist was the perfect envoy to Mexico. He once served as the U.S. ambassador to Cuba, and he spoke fluent Spanish. He was a Virginia aristocrat who was married to Thomas Jefferson's granddaughter.

William H. Prescott, Historian

Many American officers had read the book *The History of the Conquest of Mexico* by William H. Prescott, a historian and writer. Prescott was born to a wealthy family in Boston. At a young age, he lost most of his eyesight due to an accident. He traveled to Spain and researched unpublished documents about the Spanish conquest of Mexico. Because of his failing vision, someone had to read the documents to him. In 1843, Prescott published *The History of the Conquest of Mexico*, and it became a best seller. American officers marching with Scott often discussed the book as they approached Mexico City. *The History of the Conquest of Mexico* is written in a compelling, dramatic style and remains an exciting book to read today.

But Ambassador Trist had strong pro-slavery views, which made him unpopular among Polk's political foes. At first, General Scott found Trist to be arrogant and refused to speak with him. Soon, however, the two patched up their differences and worked together to reach out to Mexican authorities.

Through Trist, the United States again offered to buy California and the Northern Frontier. Trist was authorized to pay up to $30 million for the land. The offer was accompanied by a warning: either agree to the terms or Mexico City would be invaded and occupied by the American army. So far, the American military had proven to be an unbeatable war machine. Logic dictated that Mexican leadership should heed the U.S. warning.

Word came from the British Embassy in Mexico City that Santa Anna was willing to negotiate peace terms. But the Mexican general wanted bribe money for himself. This was a touchy matter because no American cared to be linked with a bribery scheme, even if it meant an end to a distasteful war. After much discussion, Scott and Trist promised Santa Anna $1 million for his personal use. The money would be payable once a peace treaty was signed. To show they were serious, the Americans sent Santa Anna a $10,000 immediate down payment. Trist later wrote that he and Scott hoped the war would come to a close with this "secret expenditure of money in Mexico."

The bribery scheme failed. Santa Anna simply pocketed the $10,000 down payment and continued the war effort. Why he acted in this manner is a matter of debate. At the time that the bribe was offered, Scott's army had been in Puebla for almost three months. Perhaps Santa Anna reasoned that the Americans were having supply problems. Despite the Mexican army's many setbacks, Santa Anna continued to believe he would eventually beat the Yankees on the battlefield. But Scott was experiencing no great supply shortcomings. He remained at Puebla as long as he did because he hoped Trist could make a breakthrough on a negotiated peace plan. When this failed to happen, Scott ordered the march to Mexico City to continue.

Some twenty miles from the Mexican capital, the American army climbed the base of the imposing volcano *Pocopocatepetl* (Smoking Mirror) and looked down at the Valley of Mexico. It was an impressive sight, similar to what the Spanish conquerors had beheld three centuries earlier. Below the mountain stretched green fields and large lakes, and in the distance the invaders gazed upon the towers of Mexico City. General Scott later wrote that the city was "the object of all our dreams and hopes—toils and dangers—once the gorgeous seat of [the Aztecs] . . . ." He then emphasized, *"That splendid city soon shall be ours!"*

On August 20, 1847, the Mexican forces put up a last-ditch stand at Churubusco, a small village six miles south of the capital. At this point, many Mexico City residents had joined the army, replacing the impoverished and dispirited draftees. For both sides, August 20 was the bloodiest day of the war. Scott's army lost 133 dead and 865 wounded. More than 4,000 Mexicans were killed or wounded, and almost 3,000 were taken prisoner.

Mexican resistance at Churubusco would have been even stronger had it not been for a feud raging between Santa Anna and a rival general, Gabriel Valencia. When Valencia's men were surrounded, Santa Anna refused to come to their aid because he wanted Valencia to be stung with the stigma of defeat. A Mexican army officer blamed the loss at Churubusco on "the stupidity committed by the disobedient Valencia . . . and the inconceivable conduct of Santa Anna when he stood by as a motionless spectator watching the ruination of his rival."

Among the prisoners taken at Churubusco was a group of about eighty-five soldiers who manned a battery of cannons and fought with outstanding bravery. When nearby units raised the white flag, they tore down the banner of surrender and urged their comrades to continue the fight. The Americans who finally captured the courageous soldiers were surprised to find that they had light skin and that some even had red hair. They were American deserters, most of them of Irish heritage, who had joined the Mexican army. The turncoats came to be called the *San Patricios*, or Saint Patrick's Battalion. Theirs was one of the many tragic stories to emerge from the Mexican-American War.

The men of the St. Patrick's Battalion switched sides for a variety of reasons. Many were lured by the Mexican offer of high pay and land grants. Others were new immigrants from Ireland who had experienced discrimination in American society. Not all the St. Patrick's men were Irish, but most were Catholics. In the United States of the 1840s, Catholics were a minority and often lived in poverty. Also prevalent among the *San Patricios* was a spiritual belief that Catholics should

never fight other Catholics. Therefore they, as loyal Catholics, must re-
fuse to participate in a war with a Catholic nation such as Mexico. The
men of the St. Patrick's Battalion were aware that the American army
viewed them as traitors. They fought as bravely as they did because if
captured they faced harsh punishments.

General Scott held the St. Patrick's men prisoner as he pondered
his next move. Scott could have marched directly into Mexico City,
but he feared he would encounter resistance from the civilians there.
Two days after the Battle of Churubusco, Scott sent Santa Anna a letter: "Too much blood has already been shed in this unnatural war between two great Republics of this Continent."

Scott proposed an immediate cease-fire to be followed by peace
talks conducted by Ambassador Nicholas Trist. Santa Anna agreed to
the cease-fire, but he was vague regarding long-term peace arrange-
ments. Still, a temporary truce was arranged. The thunder of cannons
fell silent, and peace—though fragile—prevailed between the warring
armies.

AN AVAILABLE CANDIDATE.
THE ONE QUALIFICATION FOR A WHIG PRESIDENT.

For sale at No 2 Spruce St. N.Y.

An 1848 political cartoon showing Zachary Taylor in military uniform sitting atop a pyramid of skulls, holding a blood-stained sword. The skulls and sword allude to the bloody but successful Mexican War campaigns waged by Generals Taylor and Winfield Scott.

CHAPTER 8

Peacemaking

The cease-fire began on August 23, 1847. Its terms called for all military activities to halt, but peaceful resupply of food was permitted. With resupply in mind, Scott sent a quartermaster wagon train toward the capital under officers who were ordered to buy food from city markets.

The men driving the wagons were dirty and exhausted after spending many months in the field. These were not the giants and supermen the Mexico City dwellers had feared. Instead, they were the hated *gringos*, soldiers of a nation that had waged war on Mexico and now wanted to rob Mexico of its rightful territory. The wagon train was stopped by mobs of furious citizens throwing stones and shouting, "Don't sell them food! Let the Yankees starve!"

As bitterness increased, scouts told Scott that Mexican army units were fortifying a complex of buildings called Molino del Rey. Building such fortifications violated the agreement on halting military activities. Scott ordered an attack on Molino del Rey, which lay several miles ahead of his camp. The cease-fire had lasted less than three days.

On September 8, 1847, the Battle of Molino del Rey began with a thunderous American barrage. Buildings in the complex were thick-walled and once housed a foundry. Such structures held up well under artillery bombardment. Scott ordered his infantry to charge the buildings, but because the cannon fire was ineffective his casualties were great. More than one hundred Americans were killed at Molino del Rey. "Our troops fought like heroes and were mowed like grass," said Lieutenant John James Peck.

Beyond the building complex spread the lovely wooded grove of *Chapultepec* (Grasshopper Hill in the Aztec language). In ancient times, this was a private hunting reserve for Aztec noblemen. Today Chapultepec is a park, spreading over 1,600 acres and serving as a grand playground for the people of Mexico City. In the center of the woodland rose Chapultepec Castle. This magnificent structure was built in the 1780s and was once the residence of Spanish viceroys. The castle stood on the peak of a steep hill that commanded the path leading into downtown Mexico City.

The Halls of Montezuma

A small company of U.S. Marines marched with Scott's army into Chapultepec. One Marine, whose name has been lost to history, was aware that Chapultepec was sacred grounds for the Aztecs and that Montezuma was the last Aztec emperor. The man also recalled a previous battle fought by the Marines at Tripoli in North Africa. The Marine wrote a poem with the lines "From the Halls of Montezuma/To the Shores of Tripoli," and the words now start the "Marines' Hymn," the oldest service song of the United States military.

This hand-colored lithograph published in 1847 by Nathaniel Currier shows the Military College of Chapultepec, the ancient site of the Halls of Montezuma.

Chapultepec Castle was home to the *Coligio Militar*, the national military college. About two hundred cadet students, some as young as thirteen, lived and studied there. The army moved in, and officers told the boys to leave because warfare would soon break out on the castle grounds.

According to legend, the boys refused to withdraw and instead demanded to stay and fight. The battle for the castle began on September 13, 1847, and the combat was furious. Attacking Americans placed scaling ladders against the hill and castle walls and scrambled up the ladders while under fire. The Yankees finally entered the castle, where six cadets continued to fight. One by one, five of the cadets were killed. The last cadet soldier—again, according to legend—wrapped the Mexican flag around himself and leaped off the castle wall to his death. The cadets are now hailed as the *Niños Héroes* (Boy Heroes), and they are revered in the lore of Mexican history.

The Castle Today

Since 1939, Chapultepec Castle has housed the Mexican National Museum of History. Thousands of visitors come there every day to study relics of the nation's past. Outside the buildings stands the Boy Heroes Monument, statues depicting the six courageous cadets who died defending their country.

At a clearing near Chapultepec Castle, thirty men sat on a mule-driven wagon with nooses around their necks. When an officer saw the American flag rise above the castle, he ordered the mules forward. The men fell and dangled in agony until death overcame them. They were members of the St Patrick's Brigade who had stood trial and were condemned to die by hanging. Other turncoat *Patricios* escaped death but were sentenced to hideous punishments, including being whipped with up to fifty lashes and being branded with the letter D (for Deserter) on the face. A witness to the mass whippings said of the men, "Their backs had the appearance of a pounded piece of raw beef, the blood oozing from every stripe."

The Battle of Chapultepec was the last military action of the Mexican-American War. All of Mexico City was now open to the Americans. Scott's forces entered the heart of the city, the broad plaza called the Zocalo, on September 14. The capital buzzed with anger like a hornet's nest struck with a stick. Mobs threw stones at the Americans while chanting curses. It took several days before Scott could restore order.

During the battles and the Mexico City rioting, peace talks continued. American demands had not changed. The Yankees still wanted Texas, with the Rio Grande as a border, and they insisted on taking California and all of what was once Mexico's Northern Frontier.

Santa Anna, fearing capture, fled to the Mexico City outskirts. From there, he hoped to lead a hit-and-run guerrilla war against the American occupying army. But wealthy landowners, the real power in Mexico, refused to support further warfare. Because of constant strife,

Harry Truman and the Niños Héroes

Relations between the United States and Mexico remained icy for decades after the conclusion of the war. One hundred years passed before an American president made a state visit to Mexico. In 1947, President Harry Truman broke this pattern and traveled to the United States' southern neighbor to conduct official business. One of Truman's last acts on his visit was to drive to Chapultepec Park and lay a wreath before a statue of the Boy Heroes, which stood in front of the Chapultepec Castle. The next morning, the headline of a Mexico City newspaper read: "Rendering Homage to the Heroes of '47, Truman Heals an Old Wound Forever."

Mexico was slipping into anarchy. Northern states were threatening to secede, and the Maya Indians to the south were already acting as if they were an independent people. Bandit gangs operated on the highways, making travel and commerce almost impossible. Lawlessness rose on all sides, and the landowners feared that a violent revolution would break out and strip them of their wealth and privileges.

The Mexican upper classes determined that some sort of peace treaty—even though it might be a dishonorable one—had to be hammered out. No prominent Mexican wanted his name attached to a peace treaty that so disgraced his country, but someone had to stand up and accept responsibility. The job fell to Manuel de la Peña y Peña, the head of the Supreme Court. Peña y Peña formed a temporary government in the city of Querétero, and discussions on drafting a permanent peace accord with the United States began.

In Washington, President Polk grew impatient with the delays in the peace process, and he blamed Nicholas Trist for the problems. In November 1847, the president sent Trist a letter dismissing him from his job as chief negotiator. Both Trist and General Scott were shocked by the firing, especially because it came at a point when Trist was close to concluding a final peace treaty. Scott persuaded Trist to complete the negotiations despite the wishes of the president. Trist stayed at the bargaining table, but Polk cut him from the government payroll after the firing date.

On February 2, 1848, both countries signed the peace treaty at the Mexico City suburb of Guadalupe Hidalgo. The United States was granted Mexico's Northern Frontier, land that was later called the Mexican Cession. Also, as the Americans had insisted, the Texas border was drawn at the Rio Grande. For this huge territory, the United States paid Mexico $15 million, half of what it was willing to pay just months earlier.

Bugles blew and drums rolled on the morning of June 12, 1848, as the remnants of the American army assembled on the Zocalo in downtown Mexico City. From the flagpole above the National Palace, the Stars and Stripes were struck and replaced with the Mexican Tricolor.

United States soldiers then marched out of the capital city. The Mexican-American War officially closed. By the grim arithmetic of warfare, the costs for both sides were high. The United States had lost about 25,000 regular soldiers and volunteers. Nearly 30 percent of the U.S. troops who went south to fight died there. Far more Americans perished from diseases, such as yellow fever and dysentery, than from battle causes. American survivors returned home so exhausted, ragged, and sickly that their families to the north barely recognized them.

It is difficult to calculate Mexican losses because the military kept no such records, but historians conclude that the Mexicans suffered a death rate at least three times greater than that of the American army. For the Mexicans too, diseases took more soldiers than battle deaths. Many thousands of Mexican civilians also were killed.

Mexico had lost lives, territory, and pride. The Mexican army failed to win one major battle during almost two years of warfare. A feeling of gloom hung over the country for years as the people asked why they were so completely and utterly defeated by their northern neighbor.

The Fate of Santa Anna

After the peace treaty with Mexico was concluded, the American military allowed Antonio López de Santa Anna, now a private citizen, to sail to exile in Jamaica. American officers even treated Santa Anna to a banquet before he boarded his ship. Santa Anna returned to Mexico again in 1853 when once more the country was torn by revolution. He then became president for the eleventh and final time. His eleventh term was no more successful than his previous ones, and he was again overthrown and banished to foreign exile. While living abroad, he gambled fortunes on sporting events and invested in risky business deals. He quickly ran through his great stockpile of money. Santa Anna returned to Mexico in 1874 as an elderly and impoverished man. He died two years later in Mexico City.

Mexican intellectuals understood the root cause of the nation's devastating loss: the Mexicans were not one people. Instead they were rich, they were poor; they were Indians, mestizos, and whites. Each group was jealous and fearful of the other. Therefore, they fought the Americans not as protectors of the nation, but as defenders of their own interests and the rights of their own relatively tiny factions. Writing at the time, Mexican historian Ramon Alcaraz called the conflict, "[A] theater of their victories and our disasters . . . there remained in our hearts a feeling of sadness for the evils it had produced, and in our minds a fruitful lesson of how difficult it is when disorder, asperity and anarchy prevail, to uphold the defense and salvation of a people."

The Mexican National Anthem

Hoping to boost sagging morale, the Mexican government in 1853 announced a contest to write a new national anthem. The result was the *Himno Nacional Mexicano*, which Mexicans now proudly sing at public events. It is a militaristic song, designed to erase the sting of defeat from the peoples' consciousness. The song has been compared to the *"La Marseillaise,"* the national anthem of France, which was written during the passion of the French Revolution. *The Himno Nacional Mexicano* begins with the lines:

Mexicanos, al grito de guerra
el acero aprestad y brindón.
Y retiemble en sus centros la tierra,
al sonoro rugir gel cañón.
Mexicans, at the cry of war
Prepare the steel and the steed.
And may the earth shake at its center
To the roar of the cannon.

A Forty-niner pans for gold in the American River in northern California in this 1850 photograph. During the Mexican-ruled period before 1846, the river was known as Rio de los Americanos.

CHAPTER 9

The Aftermath

Including Texas, the United States gained (and Mexico lost) almost 525,000 square miles of land. Today, it is difficult to imagine the United States without California and the southwestern states, and it cannot be foretold how that land would have fared had it stayed under Mexican control. The Mexican-American War of 1846-48 forged both countries, making them the nations we know today.

The Gadsen Purchase

In 1853, the United States bought a large strip of land that today runs along the southern parts of Arizona and New Mexico from the Mexican government. The land sale, negotiated by U.S. Minister James Gadsen, is called the Gadsen Purchase. The United States paid $10 million for 29,640 square miles. The Gadsen Purchase fixed the U.S.-Mexican borders as they stand today. Resentment against the United States remained a simmering fire in Mexico at the time of this land deal. Antonio López de Santa Anna was president during the negotiations, and uproar over the sale was a major reason why he was forced out of office soon after.

Initially, the people of New Mexico, California, and what was once Mexico's Northern Frontier noticed few modifications in their lives. Most of the men and women in this territory were ethnic Mexicans. They continued, as before, working their farms and tending to the animals on their ranches. Only rarely did they notice a new flag waving above capital cities such as Santa Fe in New Mexico and Los Angeles in California. All this was soon to change, especially in California.

On a fateful day in January 1848, a ranch foreman in the Sacramento Valley of California approached his boss, John Sutter. Years earlier, Sutter had been given a large land grant by the government of Mexico, and he created a ranch where he raised cattle. The foreman showed him some yellow specs the size of corn kernels that he had found in a streambed near where he was building a mill. Sutter asked if the specs were gold. The foreman nodded his head yes.

At first, John Sutter tried to keep the gold find a secret, but word soon leaked out and electrified nearby California communities. Flocks of villagers and farmers suddenly raced to the Sacramento region with shovels in hand believing they would dig riches from the ground. A San Francisco newspaper complained, "The whole country resounds with the sordid cry of gold! GOLD! GOLD! while the field is left half planted and the house half built. . . ." Sutter's Mill marked the beginning of the great California Gold Rush, an event that would alter history.

With the speed of the winds, word of the gold strike spread to the eastern states. Gold fever swept the country and transformed sleepy California almost overnight. In 1849 alone, some 85,000 miners, called Forty-niners, swarmed to California from the East. Very few of these Forty-niners struck it rich as prospectors, but most were young men who sought adventure as well as riches. Infected with gold fever, they flocked to camps variously called Rattlesnake Diggings, Flea Town, Whiskey Slide, and Brandy Gulch. At first, the mining camps were dens of crime and violence. Eventually the Forty-niners settled the land, and California—once an underpopulated backwater region in the Mexican empire—became the thirty-first state in the American union on September 9, 1850.

Historians have argued that events such as the California Gold Rush and a later silver strike in Nevada proved that Mexico would not have been able to keep its grip on its Northern Frontier even if there had been no war. Mexico City was too remote and the government too weak to keep control over the far-flung northern lands as prospectors and adventurers from all over the world flooded in. Manifest destiny, the historians argue, was simply written in the stars. The United States was bound to spread from sea to shining sea regardless of the will of Mexico.

Yet to this day, Mexicans feel resentment over the war and the devastating loss of territory. According to Mexican thinking, the Mexican-American War was a cruel example of a large country overpowering a smaller neighbor and stealing its land. Certainly, many Americans agreed with this sentiment. Ulysses S. Grant, the future president who served as an officer in the Mexican War, called it "the most unjust war ever waged by a stronger against a weaker nation."

Grant also said, "Nations, like individuals, are punished for their transgressions." In that statement, Grant referred to the United States being punished for the sin it committed by waging war on Mexico. The punishment came in the form of the American Civil War, one of the bloodiest conflicts in history. A root cause of the Civil War lay in the conflict with Mexico.

Slavery had long been a hotly contested issue in the United States. The acquisition of the Mexican Cession brought a new question to the arguments: should slavery be allowed in the lands opening up to the West? This new point first surfaced in 1846 when Pennsylvania congressman David Wilmot introduced the Wilmot Proviso, a measure

that would prohibit slavery in territory gained by the Mexican Cession. The proviso failed in Congress, but it triggered bitter debates that increased in rancor with each passing year. In 1860, Abraham Lincoln was elected president. Lincoln opposed allowing slavery in the new states to the west. Fearing a Lincoln presidency, southern states began seceding from the American Union. The Civil War broke out when southern troops attacked Fort Sumter in South Carolina on April 12, 1861, less than five months after Lincoln's election.

Mexico remained a country in turmoil for generations after its conflict with the United States. The nation fought its own civil war in the 1850s. It endured occupation by the French army during the 1860s. Then came a thirty-year-long dictatorship under Porfirio Díaz, and finally a bloody revolution fought from 1910 to 1920. But following the 1910 revolution, the people underwent a subtle change of thinking, one so subtle that only fellow Mexicans could truly appreciate what was taking place. For the first time in the country's history, men and women began to regard themselves as members of one nation. No longer were they Indians or mestizos; no longer did having money or living in poverty set them at each other's throats. After centuries of division, all became Mexicanos.

TIMELINE

1521	Hernán Cortés conquers the Aztecs and founds the nation of New Spain.
1608	Spaniards establish the town of Santa Fe in New Mexico; the town is the first non-Indian permanent settlement in what later will become the United States of America.
1650	Mestizos, a new race created by the blending of European and Indian bloodlines, comprise about 20 percent of New Spain's population; in the years ahead, mestizos will become an overwhelming majority.
1775	War breaks out in the United States between colonists and the government of Great Britain.
1783	The American Revolutionary War ends with the Treaty of Paris; the United States is recognized as an independent nation.
1803	The Louisiana Purchase, concluded under President Thomas Jefferson, greatly adds to the United States' territory and spurs the nation's march westward.
1810	Father Miguel Hidalgo leads an army comprised mostly of mestizo and Indian farmers in revolt against Spanish rule.
1820	Moses Austin, an American businessman, travels to Texas with plans of creating a farming community there; he dies shortly after his journey, but his work is taken up by his son, Stephen Austin.
1821	Mexico wins its War of Independence against Spain and begins a new government under General Augustín de Iturbide.
1823	Iturbide is overthrown in a revolt led by General Antonio López de Santa Anna.
1832	Sam Houston, the former governor of Tennessee, rides into Texas seeking new beginnings in his life.
1833	Santa Anna becomes president of Mexico for the first time; in the turmoil of post-independence Mexico, Santa Anna will serve as president eleven separate times from 1833 to 1855.
1835	OCTOBER 3 American settlers clash with the Mexican army in the Texas town of Gonzales.
	NOVEMBER 3 Texas leaders meet at San Felipe de Austin and form an independent government.
1836	MARCH 6 Santa Anna leads an army against Americans defending the Alamo in San Antonio, Texas; almost all the Americans are killed.

133

MARCH 27 In a battle in the town of Goliad, Santa Anna again defeats the American settlers in Texas; he executes many prisoners who had surrendered.

APRIL 21 Under the leadership of Sam Houston, a group of Texas settlers surprises and defeats Santa Anna's forces at the Battle of San Jacinto. Santa Anna is captured.

DECEMBER 7 Stephen Austin dies of pneumonia; before his death, he urged American settlers in Texas to continue their fight for independence from Mexico.

1843 In March, a militia comprised of Texas horsemen moves south of the Rio Grande, where they are captured by Mexican soldiers; Santa Anna orders one in ten of the captives to be executed.

1845 **MARCH 4** James K. Polk is inaugurated as the president of the United States; he is determined to acquire California and Mexico's Northern Frontier.

DECEMBER 29 Texas becomes the twenty-eighth state in the American union; statehood angers Mexico because that country's leaders still regard Texas as a rebellious territory.

1846 **APRIL** Mexican and American soldiers clash near Fort Texas along the Rio Grande.

MAY 8 An American army defeats a Mexican force at the Battle of Palo Alto.

MAY 11 President Polk asks Congress for a declaration of war on Mexico.

JUNE 14 American residents of California raise the Bear Flag over the community of Sonoma and proclaim California to be independent from Mexico.

AUGUST With the help of the American navy, Santa Anna returns to Mexico from his exile in Cuba; he told American leaders he would put an end to the war, but once on Mexican soil he raises an army and joins the fight.

SEPTEMBER After a bloody battle, the Americans under General Zachary Taylor occupy Monterrey in Northern Mexico.

1847 **FEBRUARY** Forces under Zachery Taylor battle soldiers commanded by Santa Anna at Buena Vista; the battle results in another U.S. victory.

MARCH An American fleet lands soldiers under the command of General Winfield Scott at Veracruz, Mexico.

APRIL   Scott's army fights Santa Anna's forces at Cerro Gordo in a battle once more won by the Americans.

AUGUST   Both sides suffer terrible casualties at Churubusco, a village just six miles south of Mexico City; a cease-fire is arranged between Scott and Santa Anna.

SEPTEMBER   Despite the cease-fire, battles break out at Molino Del Rey and at Chapultepec Castle; at Chapultepec, six young cadets, the Niños Héroes (Boy Heroes), fight to their deaths.

1848   JANUARY   A ranch foreman discovers specs of gold at John Sutter's mill in northern California.

FEBRUARY   The United States and Mexico sign a peace treaty in the Mexico City suburb of Guadalupe Hidalgo.

JUNE   The American army marches out of Mexico City.

1849   Some 85,000 prospectors swarm to California seeking gold.

1850   California becomes the thirty-first American state on September 9.

1853   Santa Anna becomes Mexico's president for the eleventh and last time.

1861   The American Civil War begins; the issue of slavery extending into territory acquired from Mexico is a leading cause of the conflict.

SOURCES

CHAPTER ONE: Independence: Triumph and Tragedy
p. 9,   "a war without mercy . . ." Justo Sierra, *The Political Evolution of the Mexican People* (Austin: University of Texas Press, 1969), 161.

CHAPTER TWO: The Northern Frontier and
               an Aggressive Neighbor
p. 25,   "our Manifest Destiny to overspread . . ." *Annals of America*, Vol. 7 (London: Encyclopaedia Britanica, 1976), 288.

CHAPTER THREE: Troubled Texas
p. 28,   "as good in every respect . . ." T. R. Fehrenbach, *Lone Star* (New York: American Legacy Press, 1968), 138.
p. 30,   "No frontiersman who . . ." Ibid., 142.
p. 31,   "to throw off their yokes . . ." Timothy J. Henderson, *A Glorious Defeat: Mexico and Its War with the United States* (New York: Hill and Wang, 2007), 59.
p. 32,   "Were I made God . . ." Hedley Donovan, ed., *The Texans* (New York: Time-Life Books, 1975), 64.
p. 36,   "A hundred years to come . . ." Henderson, *A Glorious Defeat*, 80.
p. 38,   "War is our only . . ." Fehrenbach, *Lone Star*, 189.
p. 39,   "An eagle swooped down . . ." Donovan, *The Texans* 58.
p. 42,   "I personally will march forth . . ." David A. Clary, *Eagles and Empire: The United States, Mexico, and the Struggle for a Continent* (New York: Bantam Books, 2009), 42.
p. 43,   "I can tell you . . ." Donovan, *The Texans*, 106.
p. 43,   "The first to climb were thrown . . ." Hedley Donovan, ed., *The Spanish West* (New York: Time-Life Books, 1976), 104.
p. 44,   "Houses were standing open . . ." Donovan, *The Texans*, 122.
p. 45,   "The most awful slaughter . . ." Ibid., 137.
p. 46,   "There's a yellow rose . . ." "The Yellow Rose of Texas," *Home of the American Civil War*, http://www.civilwarhome.com/yellowrose.htm.
p. 47,   "When a government has ceased . . ." Jeffrey D. Schultz, *Encyclopedia of Minorities in American Politics: Hispanic Americans and Native Americans* (Westport, Conn.: Greenwood Publishing Group), 539.

CHAPTER FOUR: Two Nations on the Brink
p. 49,   "sufficient [cause] for the immediate . . ." Henderson, *A Glorious Defeat*, 129.
p. 54,   "think of our countrymen . . ." James M. McCaffrey, *Army of Manifest Destiny: The American Soldier in the Mexican War, 1846-1848* (New York: University Press, 1992), 33.
pp. 57-60, "Mexico has passed the boundary . . ." Ibid., 7.
p. 60,   "It is a fact . . ." R. D. Monroe, "Congress and the Mexican War, 1844-1849," *Abraham Lincoln Historical Digitization Project*, http://lincoln.lib.niu.edu/biography4text.html.

CHAPTER FIVE: Warfare in Texas and Northern Mexico

p. 63,   "Lieutenant, I am General Taylor . . ." John S. D. Eisenhower, *So Far from God: The U.S. War with Mexico, 1846-1848* (Norman: University of Oklahoma Press, 1989), 36.

p. 65,   "[Our] soldiers died . . ." Clary, *Eagles and Empire*, 36.

p. 65,   "wolves [were] howling and . . ." Ibid., 114.

p. 67,   "All Mexicans have felt pain . . ." Ibid., 117.

p. 70,   "soldiers would not tolerate . . ." McCaffrey, *Army of Manifest Destiny*, 26.

p. 71,   "We honor [the volunteers] for their . . ." Ibid., 22.

p. 72,   "The majority of the Volunteers . . ." Clary, *Eagles and Empire*, 119.

p. 72,   "show us the Mexican . . ." Paul Foos, *A Short, Offhand, Killing Affair* (Chapel Hill: University of North Carolina Press, 2002), 59.

p. 74,   "Monterrey had become . . ." Clary, *Eagles and Empire*, 200.

p. 74,   "Murder, rape, and robbery . . ." Ibid., 201.

p. 76,   "[it] would probably have ended . . ." Eisenhower, *So Far from God*, 149.

p. 77,   "many [Mexican rifles] held together . . ." Clary, *Eagles and Empire*, 215.

p. 77,   "I beg leave to say . . ." Ibid., 273.

p. 78,   "The air was clear . . ." Ibid., 276.

p. 79,   "I know it, but the volunteers . . ." Ibid., 277.

p. 80,   "[They were] steeped in their . . ." Donovan, *The Spanish West*, 216.

CHAPTER SIX: The Occupation of the Northern Frontier

p. 83,   "I declared it my purpose . . ." Clary, *Eagles and Empire*, 149.

p. 86,   "I, Stephen W. Kearny . . ." Hampton Sides, *Blood and Thunder: An Epic of the American West* (New York: Doubleday, 2006), 106-07.

p. 87,   "From the Mexican government . . ." Clary, *Eagles and Empire*, 182.

p. 88,   "A more drunken and depraved . . ." Donovan, *The Spanish West*, 211.

p. 88,   "We will [kill] you . . ." Sides, *Blood and Thunder*, 175.

p. 89,   "Two of the Pueblos . . ." Ibid., 184.

p. 91,   "The field was strewn with . . ." Clary, *Eagles and Empire*, 239.

p. 91,   "visiting and conversing . . ." Ibid.

p. 95,   "a rough and barren . . ." Ibid., 231.

p. 96,   "They [the Californios] are the very best . . ." Sides, *Blood and Thunder*, 157.

CHAPTER SEVEN: War in the Mexican Heartland

p. 101,   "How horrible is the scene . . ." Clary, *Eagles and Empire*, 301.

p. 101,   "I cannot relate . . ." McCaffrey, *Army of Manifest Destiny*, 170.

p. 104,   "My heart bled for . . ." Clary, *Eagles and Empire*, 303.

p. 105,   "My duty is to . . ." Eisenhower, *So Far from God*, 271.

p. 108,   "It seemed like murder . . ." McCaffrey, *Army of Manifest Destiny*, 172.

p. 110,   "they lay thick around . . ." Clary, *Eagles and Empire*, 314.

p. 110,   "a route as complete as . . ." Ibid., 315.

p. 110,   "The troops have come back . . ." Henderson, *A Glorious Defeat*, 167.

p. 113,   "secret expenditure of money . . ." Eisenhower, *So Far from God*, 306.

p. 113,   "the object of all our . . ." Ibid., 311.

p. 114,   "the stupidity committed . . ." Clary, *Eagles and Empire*, 351.

p. 115,   "Too much blood has already . . ." Ibid., 356-357.

CHAPTER EIGHT: Peacemaking

p. 118,   "Our troops fought like . . ." Clary, *Eagles and Empire*, 366.

p. 120,   "Their backs had . . ." McCaffrey, *Army of Manifest Destiny*, 195.

p. 121,   "Rendering homage to the . . ." Jim Tuck, "Mexico's Niños Heroes ("heroic children"): reality or myth . . . .," *Mexconnect*, http://www.mexconnect.com/articles/313-mexico-s-ni%C3%B1os-heroes-heroic-children-reality-or-myth.

p. 124,   "[A] theater of their victories . . ." Donovan, *The Spanish West*, 225.

CHAPTER NINE: The Aftermath

p. 129,   "The whole country resounds . . ." Alvin M. Josephy, Jr., ed., *The Great West* (New York: American Heritage Publishing, 1982), 249.

p. 130,   "the most unjust . . ." Eisenhower, *So Far from God*, 1.

p. 130,   "Nations, like individuals . . ." Clary, *Eagles and Empire*, 421.

BIBLIOGRAPHY

Clary, David A. *Eagles and Empire: The United States, Mexico, and the Struggle for a Continent*. New York: Bantam Books, 2009.

Donovan, Hedley, ed. *The Spanish West*. New York: Time-Life Books, 1976.

———. *The Texans*. New York: Time-Life Books, 1975.

Eisenhower, John S. D. *So Far from God: The U.S. War with Mexico, 1846-1848*. Norman: University of Oklahoma Press, 1989.

Fehrenbach, T. R. *Fire and Blood: A History of Mexico*. New York: Macmillan, 1973.

———. *Lone Star*. New York: American Legacy Press, 1968.

Foos, Paul. *A Short, Offhand, Killing Affair*. Chapel Hill: The University of North Carolina Press, 2002.

Henderson. Timothy J. *A Glorious Defeat: Mexico and Its War with the United States*. New York: Hill and Wang, 2007.

Josephy, Alvin M., Jr., ed. *The Great West*. New York: American Heritage Publishing, 1982.

McCaffrey, James M. *Army of Manifest Destiny: The American Soldier in the Mexican War, 1846-1848*. New York: University Press, 1992.

Parks, Henry Bamford. *A History of Mexico*. Boston: Houghton Miffin, 1969.

Paz, Octavio. *The Labyrinth of Solitude*. New York: Grove Press, 1985.

Eduardo, Ruiz Ramón. *Triumphs and Tragedy: A History of the Mexican People*. New York: W. W. Norton, 1992.

Sierra, Justo. *The Political Evolution of the Mexican People*. Austin: University of Texas Press, 1969.

WEB SITES

http://www.pbs./kera/usmexicanwar/index-flash.html

The Public Broadcasting System's explanation of the war, told in seven parts.

http://www.lone-star.net/mall/texasinfo/mexicow.htm

The story of the war from the point of view of Texas.

http://www.mexica.net/war/Mexican-American-War.htm

Focuses on the causes of the conflict.

INDEX

PICTURE CREDITS